BURNT HONEY

by

Antonio Arreguín Bermúdez, Ph.D.

California State University, Chico

Translated by

Sara E. Cooper

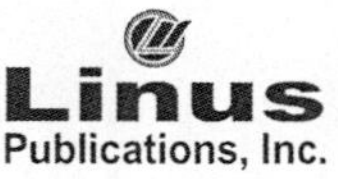

Publications, Inc.

Published by Linus Publications, Inc.

Deer Park, NY 11729

ISBN 1-934188-86-7

Printed in the United States of America.

10 9 8 7 6 5 4 3 2 1

Acknowledgements

I appreciate my colleague and friend Sara E. Cooper for all her support, her knowledge, and her dedication to the translation into English of this book, Burnt Honey. Thank you.

Thanks to June Cooper for linguistic consultation and to Elizabeth Zapata for editorial assistance.

I appreciate the infinite friendship that has been offered to me by Miguel Mendez, Rafael Franco Cuevas, Manuel Gomez, Sergio Martinez & family, and all of my colleagues at California State University, Chico. Thanks to my parents and siblings. I am grateful for all of you.

Burnt Honey seems like short stories because the order is not clear. Every chapter is something differand

- The beginning is actually the end.
- Timeless. He is just wasting his time. He isn't living or progressing, like a limbo of suffering with no purpose.
- episodes of a meaningless existence
- Follows the same characters
- Ask about Mont thing

- Poetry ↕ opposites
- Newspaper article

Mother tongue

- Different narrators
- Poetry
- News
- Progressive
- Looking Back

Dedications

I dedicate this book to my son Marco Antonio for all the nights that he sat by my side as I was writing. Also to my daughter Leah Ariana for all of her lovely "poyemas" that she would recite to me since she was very young. To my beloved wife, Anabel, thank you. Thank you for your support, your suggestions, for the work-outs, the music, and so many late nights together.

"Life is symmetrical only on the surface; perfection can't be found this side of the grave."

-Alberto Blanco-

TABLE OF CONTENTS

PROLOGUE

by

Miguel Méndez

Welcome to the Cosmos of Literature, Antonio Arreguín Bermúdez

In an ample collection of stories, whose title is *Burnt Honey*, university professor Antonio Arreguín Bermúdez tells us of the copious Mexican population, surviving in these United States, lacking any sort of legal documentation.

From his own very personal experiences Dr. Antonio Arreguín Bermúdez narrates the vision, anecdotes, and intimacies that one by one, but perhaps all stemming from a collective unconscious, create the larger tangle in which the Mexican lives his individual life.

In these brief tales, professor Antonio Arreguín Bermúdez shows literary mastery as well as a masterly knowledge of the Spanish language. Out of his literary style poetic flashes transcend the ordinary, redeeming the tragedies they convey, slavery and the poverty class, found in Latin America and points beyond, throughout this planet tat adopts us all as her global sons.

It is unnecessary to point the finger; the examples of irresponsibility are obvious; eighty percent of the population of this continent shares a miserable existence. The remaining twenty, ironically, continue to pay each other with currency and other national riches.

As you read further into *Burnt Honey*, prepare yourself to be cut to the quick by scenes of deprivation, shrouded in humiliating and painful oppression, administered by the supremely arrogant.

The undocumented Mexican people are in all truth the roots that sustain the rest of the United States population. With their walls and deportations the European Americans are only destroying themselves. Still, the Mexican proves his aching humanity in exchange for a miserable wage. Shameful and excruciating discrimination hounds him, wherever he goes.

He digs, sows, harvests, prunes fruit trees from on high, standing on rolling ladders, and for this he earns exhaustion, injuries, insults, illness, and more agonies born of racism.

The book *Burnt Honey* entertains, illustrates, and educates. The author shows us the desperate cosmos that he himself lived. He presents them through a looking glass, so as to show reality with a more absolutely revealing proximity.

Behind the dreamed-of green of the almighty dollar comes the green tinge of marijuana, the desperate desire for a woman, and insatiable physical hunger placated by lizard soups and other such tricks, in the midst of the abundant fare that the undocumented provide with their own physical degradation.

The episode in which Terrestre Mora reacts to the cruelty of an officer of the Border Control tells us much of these men and women of the earth, destined to return to the earth. He plunges in like a root, deeper and deeper, turning ineffectual those savage heaves yanking him out of the ground. In spite of everything, Terrestre Mora is that profound root, like those of fruit trees surrounding him, trees created to produce and to be harvested, but that only the forgotten and starving are able to bring to life and fully coax into complete fruition.

Far beyond his own extensive readings, Antonio Arreguín Bermúdez knows and portrays the cosmos of the modern slave, and this he does with grace and obvious literary talent. His tales capture the reader's attention, because not only are they revealing, but they also shine with an ingenious narrative artistry that by itself makes the reading worthwhile; through each dramatic and collective torment emerges a sardonic humor through which even suffering provokes a grin.

I say welcome to the book *Burnt Honey*, given to us by Linus Publications. Read it, this is art that illuminates, so swears your friend and humble servant, Miguel Méndez.

I

Burnt Honey

Here, where once stood the Ranch House, the wind still smells of burnt honey… sweet, pungent… exactly like burnt honey… For days I've been dreaming of sweet golden *buñuelos* fried in a clay kettle. Through the haze, I see a farm worker who wants to blow the harvest all to hell… that's right, all to hell…It's a little old man that I know well. I've seen him early in the morning raking the ground in slow motion; at noon he wipes his forehead with his arm and raises his eyes to the sun. Silently, he smokes a cigarette. He sadly ponders the infinite rows of cotton, and a heavy thought seems to smolder among the smoke and sweat. The old man, from right to left, from left to right, with lengths of barbed wire, goes along weaving his back to the beat, to the beat, to the staccato beat of his hoe.

In the afternoons, the old man feels like throwing himself down under a fig tree and enjoying a plate of *buñuelos* dripping sweet threads perfumed with burnt sugar. But as it hits his tongue, the sweet caramel colored gush turns into a stream of penitents mortifying their own flesh. It's death in all her living glory… that's right, death in all her living glory… That damned specter, dressed in frog skin, that stalks us in storms through towns, countryside and cities; under the sun, the rain, the wind and the cold of these lands of *Aztlán*. Our *Aztlán*.

I draw closer to the rubble of the Ranch House. With one swift kick I knock over the ashen crucifix that has shrunk to the level of my knees; right here is where they drove in Cara's cross. The scorched flight of the bees and this honeyed air make me roll through thousands of memories in mere seconds, of what used to be the Ranch House. My house, your house, our house.

The bees are unrelenting and persist in trying to build, in this very moment, a new hive in the same place their old one had been. So far the smoke rising from the old sofa has kept them from getting close enough. The poor creatures buzz and buzz about looking for the hive that so many times, on winter afternoons, had sweetened the bitterness of my existence. I dash the tears from my eyes as my memory replays scenes from the Ranch House.

* * *

This scent of burnt honey spilled through the orchards of August Ladies, Elegant Ladies, Sir Georges, White Ladies, Santa Rosas, and King's Diamonds for long years, until Mr. Glenn Jr. died. The sticky breeze was witness to the infallible death of Mr. Glenn Jr., from one hundred wasp stings spread over the pink fleshiness of his body.

In the *Fresno Bee* I read that Clemente Furia Jr. had murdered Mateo. One of the workers, interviewed by the press, mentioned that one day Mateo had come home very upset and waving around some papers that later he had hidden some place at the Ranch House. The police were looking for the papers everywhere, but never were able to find them.

Mateo had squirreled them away in the basement that for many years had protected the treasures of old Chimizú. This bundle of scribblings, written on packing paper, without dates, seems to have very little order at all, and I'm afraid that I may have made it worse as I pulled them haphazardly out of the smoking cinders at the Ranch House.

At the top of this sheet, my friend Mateo wrote that Chimizú and his wife had been placed in a concentration camp by order of the government:

His wife died in the concentration camp and he ended up diagnosed by some sociologist as mentally retarded. Chimizú drifts into view through the peach trees in this orchard of August Ladies, as if he were a ghost.

Crazy Chimizú isn't all that crazy. Here the Ranch House workers judge him because in his snarled Spanglish he says that the Ranch House is a castle. A castle? Maybe his castle? Chimizú a King? His wife a Princess? The truth of the matter is that Chimizú is the laughingstock of the workers.

Yesterday he tried to hug Cholver and Cuerna like they were his baby boys, but they blanketed his face in smoke from puffs of marijuana and then they spit on him, landing two gobs of phlegm on his bald head.

Chimizú crept off crying between the August Ladies, here and there shouting "my sons, my castle, my castle."

Years later I found out from Mateo that all of the riches that the Asian couple had hoarded had disappeared from the basement; that their agricultural equipment had been taken from the barn, and that their thousands of acres had then ended up in the hands of some Anglo ranchers.

The Ranch House belonged to Central Farm Inc., the company that employed Clemente Furia Jr. for many years. Early on the company began to use the Ranch House as living quarters for their undocumented workers. That's when the Ranch House was filled by living beings, who lived among the spirits of the dead, resting where they had been crushed underneath the shadows of history. The basement was overrun by rats and lizards, and one day the bees too began to build their hive, around the time that I first arrived here, to the Ranch House.

Through the winter evenings I would hide out from the rest of the workers and go down into the basement, where I would place a few crumbs of brown sugar close to the honeycomb. In exchange, the bees would provide me with the most delicious honey that I had ever tasted in my life. It didn't take Old Andrade very long to notice that the sugar in the cupboard was running out too fast, and he blamed Chicho and Chapo for eating it up. It made sense to blame them, since those days they had started shooting up.

Mateo was knifed here, where the other wooden cross stands, put in the ground by the workers before they left, because all of them did go. To be precise, the contractor Ramiro Ramírez took them off to live at another ranch house. It's that this company I worked for so many years, they're getting richer all the time.

* * *

The area where the Ranch House used to be is surrounded by yellow tape. I walk and walk, through the ashes, with these sheets of paper in my hand. Over there on the plank that's right by the canal, a couple of guys just put up a big sign announcing the world's biggest and most modern fruit packing factory ever built.

The workers, the bees, the Ranch House, the little outhouse, the barn, the garden, the swing underneath the fig tree, all of these trees and all of this earth of *Aztlán* have born faithful witnesses to these stories. We will all find our way onto these pages before we can be crushed beneath the shadows of the mammoth packing plant, the Central Farm Corporation Packing House of San Joaquin. That was my promise to an old friend, and that's how I want to start fighting for my people, *mi Pueblo Trabajador*.

II

The Little Clown

I left so I could see this country's land with my own eyes. The land of milk and honey. I looked around and everywhere I saw orchards of fruit trees. My eyes were about to bug out of my head from seeing so many blossoms on those trees, so perfect, so symmetrical. Such symmetry! Such perfection! Each one with five branches just so, placed in mathematical exactitude, stretching out over an endless floor of clay. Everything around me was an enormous shadow of trees dressed in white flowers, pink ones, yellow, red.

I came into an orchard and between the branches I saw a wind of colorful shadows fall over the furrows in the ground. I took off my shoes and immediately I felt myself reconnect with the earth. I felt as if my entire body was being barraged with shards of obsidian, and I felt that my heart was being pierced by the sun-drenched thrusts.

I saw the bees plunge their stingers into the center of the virgin flowers of the August Ladies trees. It was an instant of sweet pleasure for my eyes. They were mysterious insects; they were like some sort of mythical beings who lived flying among the eternity of nectar. The scent of honey was so overpowering that I felt the wax penetrating to my bones. The virginal scent from the August Ladies flowers, in that month of March, struck me in the fullness of my youth, inevitably making my sex rise.

The wind in this country, in the lands of *Aztlán*, felt like it was coming from another sky. I threw myself down headlong so I could sink my hands, my fingernails, my teeth into the earth of this Promised Land. I had my fists full of soil, in my hands I held soil, the soil from *El Norte* for the first time. It was real, it was no dream, because with my own eyes I was seeing the land that one day had offered such hopes to my parents, my grandparents, my great grandparents. Now I was there, hopes rending my heart, to make reality of the dreams sown by my ancestors. It wasn't enough to touch or squeeze this earth that had been tilled until it looked like flour. I wanted to lick it, chew it, swallow it and feel it soak in deeply into my bones. To taste it, taste it, that was it, I had to taste it so that I would believe that I wasn't on *purépecha* soil.

I bit into the earth until I could feel a ball between the roof of my mouth and my tongue. Two streams of tears flowed into my mouth, helping make a mush of soil between my teeth. With streaks of earth I anointed my hair, my arms, my chest, my manhood, and I smeared my face as if I were a clown.

The afternoon sun stretched through the mouth of a tunnel made of trees covered by swarms of flowers. Suddenly I was surrounded with the fragrance of wet earth, and then it was futile to hold back my tears. That soil tasted and smelled so exactly like the soil that made the adobe bricks of my parents' house. With the first rains of the year, the adobe of their walls emanated an aroma of earth and water that soaked into the blood-red perennials of my mother's garden until the next rainy season.

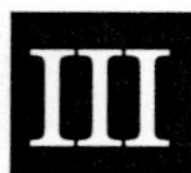

External and Internal Debt

Don't you know, Little Clown, the *migra*, the cops, or that bastard Clemente Furia Jr. could bust me any day. Now do you understand why I filled your head with ideas so you decided to learn to read and write? Don't forget that when you got to the Ranch House you didn't even know how to write the first letter of your name.

I'm hanging on to life by a thread and I'm not going to have enough time to expose the truth about my people, *mi Pueblo Trabajador*, and that's why I'm leaving you the work of bringing to life the story of the Ranch House.

You had only arrived to the Ranch House a half an hour earlier and you went out right away, because the marijuana smoke started seeping in, even through your ears, and I guess you didn't want to get high, or maybe you left because you wanted to get to know the sky in this country. There I was behind the window looking out at this little brat, wet behind the ears, clumsy and bushy like a malnourished rat. Your face was pale, but without a single zit. You were surprised to see so many trees all around you and you had no idea which way to go, because this Ranch House is like a deserted island if you look at it from up on top of that wooden cross that sticks out of the skylight in the living room. I say skylight as a joke, because in reality it's just a hole in the ancient ceiling of this house.

Silvino and Rosalío, may they rest in peace (if peace exists), built that cross that sticks through the ceiling. Between the two of them they nailed it together, here, in the living room, before I got here or ever met them.

At the border I met an old friend from seminary on the street, who now was a priest in the city, and right in front of the *coyote* he asked me why I had abandoned my studies at the seminary. I wish he had never opened his mouth, because the *coyote* who was getting me across the border went on blabbing about it all through Los Angeles. He wouldn't stop fucking with us! He fucked and fucked with us until he got the thousand dollars for each chick he brought across. He would tell each of the bosses that they should have me listen to their chicks' confessions and that I should give them my blessing so the *migra* wouldn't nab them before they paid up what they owed them. Most of us were looking for the lands of *Aztlán*, *El Norte*, to escape the external debt of our own country, and when we got to *Jauja* they saddle us with another debt and these bastards, here on this side of the border, they'll take a pound of flesh out of your heart if you don't make good.

What a fucked up scene! The chicks in the *coyote's* corral. The *coyotes* selling their prisoners to other savage beasts, it's almost like watching monsters devouring each other. An endless chain that drags us across the damned clay of the border, a border that the *gringos* painted across our own patio.

On thousand, two thousand, three thousand dollars for passage with a *coyote*. You get here and you can't find work and when you do the foreman starts jotting down everything in his little book: rent, water, electricity, cigarettes, food, and even marijuana, whether or not you ever smoke it. The dictatorship isn't over yet, my friend.

I'm telling you, Clown, we come from our mother's womb branded with the external debt. Goddamn fucking external debt!

I am the external debt in the middle of two countries. Systemic injustice has not yet ended in Mexico or in Jauja. We're still living the era of feudalism. The time of the landowner still goes on, perennial through the years. Aztlán: pray for us, your faithful pilgrims. We ask for your blessing. Protect us. Through the centuries of the centuries.

We are screwed and I mean screwed. Fucked! We are going to be drugged to the gills. But now even crying won't do us any good, my friend.

We cry and cry when we come into this world, and what does it get us? It's a jolting transition from the womb to searing debt. At least we ought to get a cushion of water. Black waters? Then we wouldn't only be born drugged, but drooling as well, with Coca-Cola written all over our face. And I'm not talking about the Tormes River, like *Lazarillo*, but at least a pond of stagnant water. But in any case we wouldn't be the children of rape and pillage, that is, children of our good and fucked mother, and we would go on to be children of our Stagnant Mother.

Our own sweet mother is the only one who wants to protect us, who presses us between her bleeding thighs. Her husband squeezes her hand, then slips away from the bloody scene. He paces from one side to the other trying to look nervous. What a pretty act! Really he's thinking about how many days he's going to have to go without sex. Passing through his thoughts are Cuca, Tere, or even the godforsaken Pascualita who, besides being cross-eyed, drools.

No sooner does the little head appear and the midwife or the gynecologist yanks us out like we were a cork in a bottle. We're just one more number, and with an oversized pair of scissors in her hand, the midwife glances at the sun and the gynecologist at her wristwatch and then they look at the mother impatiently, while she lovingly lays her baby on her lap.

Wrapped in blue swaddling you are to your father a little man, look at what a strong little guy he is, or otherwise maybe a priest or a monk, or who knows what. Wrapped in pink, there the mother gets a hand in, but how her father sweats until the day he can finally breathe a sigh of relief to see his little girl married in white at the altar of the church.

IV

Etchings of Clay

In the corral outside the house, beneath the thick shadow of the jacaranda, my mother gave me her blessing, after she had finished putting her daubs of clay on the kitchen floor. But they were more than just smears of mud that my mother was adding to the bedroom, the hallway, the entryway and the kitchen. They were etchings of clay beings with enormous eyes painted onto the clay ground, beings that scared me at night. I always heard my mother say, I need to refinish the floor at the front door, and in the kitchen too, and…My mother expressed her creative genius with hands gifted in mixing clay for sculpted artistry. I always remember her kneeling on the floors carpeted with clay, wearing a clean apron over dresses that she made herself.

How many beings were there under the newest one? This feathered serpent is mine, I told her one day after she had just refinished the patio. The fresco dried quickly so I could play with my feathered snake on the floor. One day I came back from the back yard, I had just caught a grasshopper among the blood-red perennials, and I started crying because the feathered serpent was gone. He had slithered away. One day he'll come back, from over there, where the dawn breaks drenched in blood, don't worry, my mother told me.

My mother explained to me that the earth devours everything.

"It gives us life and it gives us death."

"Did the earth gobble up my feathered serpent?"

"Yes, it ate him up, but some day he will come back. From over there, where the sun rises."

The next day before I got up, my mother had patterned an enormous grasshopper in the same place where my feathered serpent had been.

I always remember my mother gazing at her art. Sitting down, she would sigh beside the water cistern that nestled among the scarlet blooms. Her sigh, after she settled into the wicker chair, filled her face with joy at the sight of her art: serpents, jugs, tigers, jaguars, corn, flowers, moons, suns.

"The pyramids in the entryway came out really nicely," my mother said as she dried her hands on her apron. "The temples of the sun and moon are pointing toward the north, that's where this wretched cold is coming from, my dear boy. Up there life shrivels up, it dries up. In the damned *Norte* your father worked away his best years while I was here waiting, weaving my life away."

My father, close to his team of mules, was chopping a mesquite trunk into firewood. My mother called for him to come and say goodbye to me. He kept on hacking away at the firewood and seemed not to have heard her. In one stroke of the axe he splintered the heart of the log, and sheared off a thick sliver that pierced the white mule's chest like a bull's-eye. The mule started to pull out of her halter and kick out at her companion, a mule so black she was almost purple. The white chest and front legs were bathed in blood. My father ran to the kitchen for a fistful of granulated salt. He got back and crept up to the animal with his hand held out in front of him, carefully, to try to calm her down little by little.

"That's right, there you go my beauty," he murmured to soothe her.

My father got closer and closer with that fistful of salt in his right hand, trying to take hold of the reins to quiet her down. At first the mule was skittish and wouldn't let him get close enough. He caressed her back, her mane, and then in one motion he thrust his fingers into her breast to pull out the sliver of wood. He jerked out his fingers, bloody flames, and rubbed a poultice of salt over the mule's ripped flesh. He tossed the sliver to the ground and pulled out his handkerchief to wipe off his hand and swab his forehead.

My mother hugged me close and asked my father to give me his blessing.

"Christian, give your son your blessing before he goes away *al Norte*," my mother begged him.

Without saying a word my father looked at me and went off walking slowly toward the house. My eyes followed him and I saw him take a chair off of the porch and place it next to a cotton thistle plant that was right by the stone enclosure. He called me over and asked me to stand with my back to the chair and close my eyes. I stood in front of the chair and closed my eyes, and then he ordered me to sit down in the chair but keeping my eyes closed. I obeyed him, and when I sat down I fell back onto the thorny bush. My father had moved the chair away. I cried out in pain and my mother in anger.

"Jesus, Mary and Joseph! Why did you go and do that, Cristián?" I heard her ask him.

"This is so you learn to not trust anybody or anything in this life. Don't even trust your own father in this hellhole of a world, you stupid boy. Up their in *El Norte*, you're going to have to grow some claws," my father warned me as he wiped the sweat off his brow with his red handkerchief.

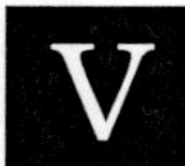

The Cherry Beams

It was getting dark as we came down through Grape Vine. Highway 99 felt like a snake burning and burning between the orchards of the San Joaquin Valley. We pulled into Delano to get gas, and the coyote called the foreman Clemente Furia Jr. to see if he needed any workers. The boss asked for eight arms.

"I'll bring you a little monk out there, you bastard," the coyote said over the phone.

The day I arrived at the Ranch House, Silvino and Rosalío asked if I would say mass in the living room on Sundays, but Old Andrade told them that I was an atheist monk. "A what!" they yelled, shocked into silence. "Yes sir. A monk that doesn't believe in God." They couldn't believe what they were hearing and the two cried all Saturday night and halfway through the next morning.

They started crying again the next weekend, but this time their tears were for something else. They were crying because that's the day they crucified Cara. Over there by the fig tree he scrambled up on top of the roof to get good and fucked up, like he used to say.

All of us want to climb up high and be able to escape someday from this damn misery. That's right, escape our home, family, town, country… Escape ourselves… You have to learn to hate your house and you have to get it through your head that your worst enemy is your own self. That's right, we have to hate our own home so that we can get away from it. Hate it… hate it… hate ourselves… and then fly… fly… flyyy….

Cara loved to climb up those cherry beams because he said that he felt like he was leaving this life of clay behind him. Only he knew where he was going. Silvino and Rosalío would make the sign of the cross at him when they saw him climb up to take his trips at the top of those cherry beams.

"God's gonna punish that boy. How dare he smoke his weed somewhere as sacred as the sacred Holy Cross of Our Lord Jesus Christ," said Rosalío as he was watching Cara roll up some of the dried herb into a paper.

"I'm going to get on board the plane, you crazy sons of bitches," said Cara. "I'm gonna paint up a bit of this fucking fantasy life. I'll be seein' ya on the steps tomorrow, you bastards!"

The dried-up cherry tree was just one tree less for the owner of the orchard, an insignificant loss. But it had to be replaced immediately, and all he had to do was wag his finger before Clemente Furia Jr. started wagging his jaws and we started planting his new little tree. The owner's labor costs were nothing, because Furia would order us out saying go to such and such lot and pull out all the dried trees that you find there. You can bring them here and use them for firewood. Any wood we found we brought it back because we knew how it gets bitching cold in the San Joaquin Valley.

Other times, on our day off, Furia would show up with the saplings ready for transplanting and he would say, go out to such and such lot, the Santa Rosas. The old man will let you have all the firewood, but he wants you to plant these right in the same spot.

For Silvino and Rosalío, the dried Santa Rosa cherry wood erected in the living room became a symbol of their religious beliefs; for the orchard owner, it only meant that bad pruning was affecting his harvest; and, for Cara, the cherry beams turned into fodder for his trips.

Cara climbed up the rough trunk, got himself comfortable on the thick horizontal bough, and started lighting up joints. From way up there he said that this land looked like the film of algae that grew on the surface of the canals in his hometown. Cara was showing off up on the makeshift cross, which had been tied together with baling wire that Silvino and Rosalío had soldered. The boss, don Clemente Furia Jr. offered him a line if he would stand up on the horizontal beam of the cross. Cara was able to stand up there on one foot without much trouble. Some of the guys laughed, spraying drink and spit up at him and the others applauded his agility on the cross. Furia tossed him a little mirror, a Gillette razor blade and a little envelope of white powder. Cara measured out a line of snow on the mirror, pulled out a straw from his pants pocket, and in one snort inhaled the entire line. The boss offered him two more if he could stand on one leg on top of the vertical beam of the cross. Cara tried to, lost his balance, and his body fell like lead onto the sharp point of the Santa Rosa. It split his guts wide open, beginning the end of his eternal flight.

Since then, nobody wanted to take down the mirror, or that stake driven into the heart of the living room, because right there Cara had carved his initials.

The mirror with its powder has turned into a shrine for Cara. The boys make sure that it always has a little pile of snow, so our friend Cara can live flying forever.

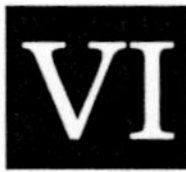

Cholver and Cuerna

That night, to go to sleep I curled up in a corner of the Ranch House. I was too excited to sleep a wink all night long. At dawn I was going to be in the middle of a peach or cherry orchard with a 12-foot ladder and thus would I begin to earn my first dollars.

I heard that knocking off the green fruit from the trees, the Elegant Ladies, White Ladies, June Ladies, August Ladies, Luxury Ladies, Summer Ladies, Diamond Kings, Sir George and Summer Brilliants, was the easiest work that we would have all year. It was a matter of pruning branch by branch so as to leave four or five little green fruits, according to the size of the tree and the size of each branch.

By order of the boss Clemente Furia Jr., the most veteran workers were going to teach me how to thin out the fruit trees. They said that Cholver had gone off to grab some branches with green fruit from the cherry and peach trees in a couple of orchards that were real close to a little grocery store called Wetbacks' Market.

Cholver took more than three hours to get back, because at the crossroads the Border Patrol was stopping all the farm trucks and vans. Cholver stayed hidden in an orchard until the INS filled up their dog cages with undocumented farm workers. Cholver told us that they had stopped three panel trucks filled to bursting with *braceros* so they met their quotas fast.

When he finally arrived at the Ranch House, Cholver had some cigarettes and a six-pack of beer. Rufas chewed him out because he spent all the money that Rufas had given him to buy a package of tortillas and a dozen eggs.

"Shut the hell up, fucking Rufas! When they hand out our first check I'll pay you back your ten bucks. If you had seen how the fucking *Migra* was dragging three ladies that didn't want to get into the paddy wagon. It made me so mad to see how they just shoved them in, ignoring their crying and kicking. It made me so goddamn pissed off to see that and that's why I spent your fucking money on this beer," Cholver told his friend Rufas, putting on show of being angry. Rufas looked mad, but smiling between gritted teeth he walked away, resigned.

Cholver showed me the branches he had just cut and started to explain to me how to thin them out. Cuerna grabbed one of the branches out of his hands because he wanted to be the one that showed me how to thin the fruit. Cuerna got up on the only chair that we had in the entire house to hang a piece of string from the ceiling and then he tied one of the branches to the end of the string about at eye level. With his fingers he pulled off fruit from the branch until he left it with only six tender baby peaches spaced equally from each other.

"You leave five or six little fruits. It all depends on the size of the branch, because if it's bigger then you can leave one or two more. And if…" Cuerna never got to finish his explanation because his friend Cholver butted in.

"Hold on just a minute," Cholver said to his buddy Cuerna, smiling a little. "You think that you're going to know more than I do. You've got to tell this little dude which fruit you leave and which you throw out. The runts you never leave them, and the biggest ones you always want to leave them. It's like the guys in Tijuana that clear away the old whores. When a whore gets so old and ugly that it leaks out her eyes, so she's not worth a damn, to hell with her! I suppose that when you got here all they told you was to leave five or six fruits on each branch and that was it."

"Shut your trap! Shut up! Nobody never taught me to thin out, or to prune, or any other damn thing," Cuerna shouted angrily.

"Hold on just a minute, remember that I taught you how to pick table grapes in Parlier," Cholver stuck in.

"You're crazy! I got here to *Califas* before you did. Dude, don't pay any attention to him. He's already drunk," Cuerna said to me, ignoring his friend.

Cholver and Cuerna kept on drinking as they were trying to explain to me the ins and outs of thinning fruit trees. They couldn't get on the same page. Cholver would tell me how to do it one way, then Cuerna would tell me to do it a different way. After a long while, the two veteran farm workers, seventy-something years old and still single, ended up crying and remembering the girlfriends they had left behind in Mexico more than have a century ago. The two had come to the United States when they were barely fourteen years old and they had never been able to go home.

I've heard say that during the season of thinning out the fruit you could earn up to two hundred dollars a week, take home, after they took out deductions for who knows what. Something called state tax, federal tax, and social security. Social security? What was a social security? It was the first time I heard anybody say social security.

I couldn't get settled in my improvised cardboard bed and maybe that's why I couldn't get to sleep. I stuck my hand in my pants' pocket to try to find the little plastic card case that my grandfather had given me before I left. There it was, the little case with its two little cards, one with a picture of the Virgin of Guadalupe and the other a blue one with nine numbers on it. My grandfather told me that those numbers on the card were good ones that the United States government had given him to be able to work after he had fought in a war.

"I was going up to the North, supposedly to work in the fields. I was expecting to see watermelons the size of a pig and what I saw were bombs the size of a lamb. They wanted them to use the bombs on those people with the squinty eyes, some country full of folks that were fighting with the United States. And before you could bat an eye I was drafted and shipped out of some city… how the hell do you say, it starts with the letter… I think it was Texas," my grandfather would go on about his experiences in the United States, especially when he had been drinking his liquor.

My grandfather always had talked a lot about the part that he had played in some war in some other country. He talked a lot too about when he and my dad were *braceros* in the lands of *Aztlán*. My grandpa said that working in the fields of *Aztlán* was awful hard, and that it was better to waste your time in Mexico, with your family and on your own lands even if it was piece work. He said that over on the other side people who lived by God's grace turn into starving animals and that little by little your belly gets filled up with balls of hate and suffering, drenched with misery.

"Even if yer a real man, well truth is when yer on your own you feel like bawlin' like a baby because the years just eat away all yer hopes and dreams. Little by little yer belly starts to swell up with those balls of bitterness and that's when you start leaking out blood even through yer eyeballs," my grandpa would tell me sitting in his chair, where he would be mending some shoes, as I contemplated the air of sadness in his every movement.

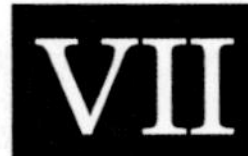

Ramplas

I couldn't get comfortable in the corner I had picked out to sleep in my first night at the Ranch House. The wood was hard and the cardboard didn't make a good mattress. I wanted to sleep but I couldn't, I was so excited and so nervous because it was already almost four in the morning. I sat up to move one of the pieces of cardboard that was poking me in the ribs and I realized that there were eight of us workers laying down on that floor.

In one corner of the room another guy was awake. He saw me and told me his name was Ramplas. On the headboard of his bed of cardboard, which was the wall, he had the Virgin of Guadalupe drawn in pencil. Ramplas took out a match and he lit the wick of a votive candle that was burned down half way. He leaned back onto his cartons and told me that I would get used to my fellows' foul smelling snores that stank of beer and marijuana.

"As soon as you start working, you're gonna be able to sleep just fine. You'll see! There's no better bed than being good and tired," Ramplas told me, yawning.

In less than three minutes Ramplas had fallen to sleep and started to snore. I hadn't paid any attention before to the snores of the other workers. I hadn't even noticed the stench that emanated from those snores and all the shoes that had been left at the head of each worker's bed.

I stayed there lying down without being able to drift off. I had my ear flat against the cardboard. I started hearing noises underneath the floor of the house. I wanted to fall asleep, but I couldn't. I didn't know if it was the snoring, the stench, or the noises from underneath the house that kept me so awake in that first night at the Ranch House. I think that what kept me up was my yearning to get to work. I wanted for it to be daybreak right away because in just one day I would earn thirty or thirty five dollars. I wanted so bad to send my parents five hundred dollars all together. I couldn't even imagine how happy their faces would be when they got it. I wanted to send them a lot of money so they would have enough to buy corn and beans. More than anything else I wanted to send them money so that they would send my little brothers and sisters to school. I had promised my big sister that I would send her enough to buy her books and uniform for high school.

Later I would start saving up to buy a brand new car and to build a brick house for my parents. Then my mother could stop spreading layers of clay over the floors and walls, and my father would stop worrying about the leaks in the roof during the rainy season. I was tired of listening to my mother pray to gods and saints for rain. She would pray to *Tlalóc* and the Virgin of Guadalupe for it to rain so that the beans and corn plants would grow, and then she would pray to God for it to stop raining so much because of the rain leaking in all through the house.

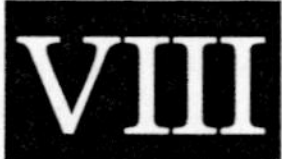

Roaches

The clock struck four in the morning and I still had not slept a wink the entire night. Mmmm… My first day on the job in *El Norte*. At four thirty the workers who were asleep in the room started stretching on the cardboard that they used as beds. I felt like I was finally falling asleep just when we had to get up. Ramplas was the first one to get up and the first one to let out a fart. Then the farts started flying so fast that I got up right away and went into the living room because I couldn't stand the disgusting odor.

In the living room there were other workers resting on cartons and covered with old blankets. Old Andrade snatched the blankets off to wake them up. With his hoarse voice sounding like an ancient alarm clock, he yelled at all of us that it was time to get the hell up.

In the living room, Old Andrade lit up a Marlboro, threw the match out the window with a broken plane and went into the kitchen to boil water to make instant coffee. I followed him in because I couldn't stand the stink of feet and farts in the main room. When I came into the kitchen you could hear something crunching underneath our shoes. I felt like I was stepping on popcorn. Old Andrade turned on the kitchen light and I realized that what we were stepping on were cockroaches. They weren't the stumpy roaches or the flying ones that I had seen before, they were little bitty roaches that ran real fast. They looked like little bumper cars like the ones they would bring in on December 12 for the Guadalupe Ranch Festival.

I stood in a corner of the kitchen, shaking, watching a swarm of roaches boil over on the stove. Old Andrade used some pliers to turn on the gas on two burners and standing back lit a match and tossed it over close to the pilot light. A flower of blue and yellow flames opened up at each burner. Old Andrade laughed at the roaches scorching their stinking hind ends in the petals of the flames. The reek became unbearable and I figured I'd better leave.

Some of the workers were washing their face at the spigot outside of the house. Others were over in the August Ladies orchard taking care of business. Old Andrade came out with a pewter pot of coffee in his right hand and his Marlboro in the other. As a joke, Old Andrade asked Cholver to unzip his pants because he needed to take a piss. Cholver, who woke up with a hangover, walked off irritated and went to rinse out his mouth with water from the spigot.

At exactly five o'clock in the morning the boss Clemente Furia Jr. came for us. He pulled up in a Ford van, blue, a brand-new one. He had on an army jacket and dark, dark glasses. He had a stare like a pistol and a Rigo Tovar hairdo.[1] Burning rubber, he turned around in the Ranch House patio. We all ran to get up into the van. Inside the van already were María, Gertrudis, Pedro Coras and Rufas.

I don't know how, but we fit twenty workers inside that van. We were standing up side by side like a packet of matches. I was scared because the boss said that we had to go the back way because the Border Patrol was at the intersection of Mountain View and Frankwood Avenue. After almost an hour on the road we got out to thin out an orchard close to Sanger.

I had no sooner gotten out of the van when I was struck by the peach orchard. I didn't see a single weed in the whole orchard. I didn't see bitter greens, clover, thistles or birds pecking at the morning. I didn't hear the moos of the cows tied up in the corral. This land was so different than the cornfields of Michoacán! I remembered the rows of corn in my parents' fields. I was struck with a memory of the thicket and the red fish among the reeds of the Lerma River.

The contractor showed up with the twelve-foot ladders. There were thirty five ladders and we were only twenty workers. Clemente Furia Junior ordered Chico and Chapo to set up the fifteen extra ladders further out in the orchard.

---

1 Rigo Tovar: A popular Mexican singer and performer of the 1980s, blind, who was famous for his long wavy hair and dark glasses. From Matamoros, Tamaulipas, Tovar died in 2004 in abject poverty, his manager having fled with his entire fortune.

The job of thinning the fruit seemed easy to me, even fun, but I still couldn't help being nervous. "Why should I run away from the law?" I asked myself. I think if the Border Patrol showed up, I wouldn't run away. Why should I run away from another human being? Maybe the fear of being deported would make me run. Make me afraid of another live person. The dead are already dead and what can they do to you, my mother would say to me when before bedtime I would refuse to walk the path through her blood-red perennials to fetch a pot of water. My mother knew that it wasn't dead or live people I was afraid of. I was afraid of the clay figures that she had scratched into the floor of the house and that I was sure came to life at night.

Clemente Furia Jr. came to look over the work I was doing from time to time. I only needed to watch how the others were doing the thinning to learn how to do it, but there was always some excuse for Furia to yell at me, "You're cutting off too much, you're leaving a lot of little runts, get those fingers moving faster."

Time sped by punctuated by continuous cussing, "retard, idiot, I'm fucking your sister, suck me, jerk me, your grandma, yours, yours is mine, it's a bitch, fuck my mother, fuck yours..." The clock struck twelve and I started getting hungry. What were we going to eat? Two o'clock came and in the banquet of bad words nobody said one word about food.

The contractor brought us water in a 20-litre plastic jug. On one of the handles was tied a dirty and bent aluminum cup. The boss gave us ten seconds to get down the ladder and take a drink. If we took longer than the ten seconds he started cursing our mothers.

"You son of a fucking, bearded, street-running, fruit-picking whore, making a fool of himself drinking water," he would yell at us, laughing.

I had come up running to drink water and I had barely brought the cup to my lips when I heard Clemente Furia Jr. cussing out me and my mother. I drank barely a half-cup of tepid water. A half hour later I started needing to piss but I didn't dare ask the boss for permission. I didn't know if you could do that kind of thing in this lovely land, so free of weeds, or if there was a latrine nearby. I thought about pissing beside the tree that I was working on, but I didn't do it because I remembered Maria and Gertrudis. I hadn't seen any of the workers take a piss. Maybe I was going to have to hold it until we finished working. Finally I couldn't hold it any more and I asked Clemente Furia Jr. for permission to go and take care of it.

"Get the lead out!" Don Clemente told me. "That's why I don't want y'all drinking water, because you spend all day pissing like donkeys with an infection."

I went to piss over at the vineyard next to the orchard. And Maria and Gertrudis? Would they pee right there in the orchard? I went back to work and the boss chewed me out but good.

"You little bastard, you must have a big one if you had to go all the way to the fucking vineyard to piss," the boss Clemente Furia Jr. told me, as he unzipped his pants to go on the tree where Maria was working.

He already had cussed out Maria and her mother six times or so for leaving scrawny buds on the tips of the branches. He barely ever talked shit about Gertrudis' mother, but he did tell her off her once in a while for using only one hand to do the thinning. She would hold on to the branch with her left hand and work with the other. She wasn't the only one who was doing it. We all were doing it so we didn't fall when we were reaching for a branch higher up.

"You look like a fucking parrot!" Clemente Furia yelled at Gertrudis as she was trying to reach one little branch. "You spend your whole time grabbing that stick. Didn't you get enough last night, you bitch?"

He shook her ladder, which made her cry out, terrified. She barely avoided falling down from half-way up the tree. Nobody said a word. You could hear perfectly as the little green peaches shaken loose fell against the wood of the steps and then the softer thud as they hit the loose earth. Through the rain of little green balls you could make out Maria's sobs. Why were those two women working for Clemente Furia Jr.? Why did they look at each other so hatefully? Why did the boss treat them as if they were his property? Why would he flirt with the two of them, and then walk all over them, like a rooster with his hens? Maybe they were his lovers, his girlfriends, his whores.

I could tell that it was close to five in the afternoon, and nobody knew when we were going to stop working. Only Clemente Furia Jr. knew. The boss asked Chicho to come down so they could smoke another joint. The foreman would share it with his buddies and no one else.

My first day of work among the June Ladies ended at six in the afternoon. With our tongues hanging out we put away the ladders and returned hungry to the Ranch House.

IX

Give Us This Day Our Daily Joints

Clemente Furia Jr. pulled out of Maria's purse seven joints and threw them out the van window. Maria jotted them down in the boss's ledger. Bastard! One day I'll make you pay for all of your fucking injustice, I imagined telling him as I washed my face at the water spigot. I wanted to scream right in his face and tell him that I wouldn't pay him a nickel for his shitting marijuana that was filling the workers with poison.

Chicho and Chapo ran to pick up the joints. They called over the other workers and everybody sat in a circle, except for Old Andrade and Little Clown, the recent arrival. To tell the truth, nobody knew Little Clown's real name and nobody cared. He's a boy about fourteen years old and today, his first day on the job, they gave him the nickname Little Clown, to give him a hard time. They offered Little Clown a toke, and without opening his mouth he shook his head no. He retreated to the miniscule and windowless bathroom to shower with the water hose. The boy must have been hungry and without a doubt he was thinking about eating while he was bathing. He still doesn't get it that those marijuana cigarettes are going to be the only dinner he gets after working straight through twelve hours thinning the fruit trees. In two more weeks he'll find out that he has to cover his part of the cost of the joints that the rest are smoking today, just like the joints they'll smoke tomorrow, the next day, and the ones after that. He'll end up like the rest of them. I remember when Chicho and Chapo got here. The first five days they refused to smoke pot but now they're a couple of stoners and they even shoot up once in a while.

Little Clown's black hair and juvenile face have made me think about how old the rest of us are getting. I turned around to look at the Oaxacan's ugly face, Chapo's tousled ashy hair, Melquiades' disgusting beard, Scarface's bad eye. I saw pairs of lifeless eyes in my fellows' grey faces and I noticed the rags that I was wearing.

I ended up staring at Squirrel, who had leaned back against some blankets blackened with filth. Now he seemed to me smaller, toothier, and he looked to me like the little animals that spend their days building underground labyrinths. The Mute was acting more like a real deaf-mute every day. The Parrot chatters more every day, going on and on about stupid shit. The white clouds covering Pinto's neck and hands were spreading more and more. Old Andrade wastes all of his time speaking to the earth as if it could understand him. Everybody I work with, myself included, are acting and looking more and more like our alter ego. Kalimán has started wearing a turban and when he's puffing on the joint he says, "Vatos, serenity and patience, plenty of patience."[2] Now I ask myself existentialist questions.

I left the seminary. Of course, my father and grandmother were distraught. They should have let me decide whether I wanted to go into a seminary and be a monk or not. But no. Just because they wanted to have a man of the cloth in the family. I don't deny that at first I liked the idea of going, so I could have the chance to read as many books as I wanted from all those that would be right at my fingertips. But it wasn't like that. We read only selected books, mortified our flesh with lashes every night, "as said and ordered by God's word," and then there were the sins. Fifteen years old, and I couldn't even jerk off for the fun of it, because I always saved it for right before confession so I would have sins to confess.

I wanted to go out and see the world, and without knowing what I was doing I found myself trapped in this miserable world, lost between the long shifts at work. It's a hard struggle, but not impossible, what we farm workers in the United States are up against. Some day the people in the White House, when they bite into a sweet Sir George or a juicy Santa Rosa cherry, they'll remember us pickers, when they see our art in their museums. The art of the men and women of clay, art formed from the earth, earth turned into art. They will be shocked when they see muddy figures with two hairless peaches as testicles on a plate of clay and they will utter their favorite exclamation, "Oh my God."

---

2 A character from a serialized Mexican comic, Kalimán the Incredible Man fought evil with his special mental powers. Created by Rafael Cutberto Navarro Huerta and Modesto Ramón Vázquez González in 1965, Kalimán's signature dress included a turban, and he preached an attitude of tolerance, tranquility, and serenity in the face of crisis and adversity. His official website is http://www.kaliman.net/.

They call me Atheist because I draw saints smoking pot, virgins pruning trees as they climb ladders that go up to heaven, and gods that cross the border without legal work permits. I don't want my nickname to make people think I'm an unbeliever. I do believe! I believe in truth and I see the reality of what we are for the gringos and the bosses, arms without a brain and dark strange beings that do manual labor six days a week and rest on Sundays, drunk on shitty Coors and Budweiser. But maybe I don't believe! That's right. I don't believe in the truth according to Furia and Ramirez, that we can't even go to the supermarket; claim unemployment, medical coverage, or retirement; or get our own Social Security card.

We run the risk of not getting back to work if we go to buy potatoes and flour. In the Town & Country supermarket the INS hunt us like lions hunt deer at the stream. You've got to be devious to trick the gringo gods, like Andrade does with his fresh-laid eggs.

The other day, Old Andrade squatted down beside the water spigot. He reached into his jacket pocket and pulled out a raw egg. He brought it to his ear and shook it gently to make sure it wasn't rotten. The egg was still good. He had hidden the egg along with half a dozen more in a sand pit among the Santa Rosas, on the other side of the canal. He cracked the shell with his bottom teeth and emptied the viscous liquid into his mouth. He took a few grains of salt out of his pocket and swallowed them as if he had just done a shot of tequila. He tossed the eggshell out into the weeds and blew his nose into his sleeve. Little Clown watched him closely, without blinking an eye.

To one side of Old Andrade were Chicho, Parrot and the Oaxacan, asleep on the ground. They had their faces covered with some old blankets.

"Around here they try to fool their empty stomachs by sleeping," Andrade said to Little Clown. "Look at them! Bastards! They cover their faces to fake out their hunger."

At nine o'clock at night Little Clown fell asleep on some cardboard cartons. In his hands he held a few green peaches. Before he drifted off I saw him roll them around in his fingers as if they were marbles. I so wanted to tell him, "Don't go to sleep, because you haven't eaten anything all day. Look, I have here a little money I saved, let's go to the gringos' store to buy a liter of milk and some bread so you can eat." But I didn't do it, and if I did it tomorrow, I would just be keeping him from getting used to how life really is. I hope he manages to survive two more days without eating, maybe three, until the boss gets the fucking urge to pay us.

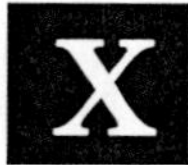

Camouflage

The foreman Clemente Furia Jr. woke up in a real bad mood today, worse than usual. He was cussing us out all morning long. He threw a punch at Maria and gave her a black eye. He took hold of her hair and dragged her along the earth.

"Cleme, Cleme, let go of me, please!" yelled Maria, "Let go of me, you bastard!"

He let her get up and then with another punch laid her back on the ground. Gertrudis was thrilled by the whole thing.

The workers were so silent that you could hear the hard little green balls falling down the ladders and our empty stomachs growling.

It was my third day and I still hadn't tasted the food of this country. I wanted to try the taste of tortillas, milk and bread. I was curious about what the stores here would be like. Would they sell jalapeño peppers fresh or just pickled in the can? Would they sell lard by the ounce? And dollars, what were they like? I still hadn't even seen a dollar bill. I wanted to know if the gringos sent their youngest kids to buy them cigarettes or beer so they could buy a couple candies with the change.

I wanted so bad to drink one of the soft drinks from El Norte, to eat some candy. I wanted to meet *gringos* and *gringas* in person. I wanted to see how they dressed and hear how they spoke English. If these were their orchards, where were they, and why weren't their children playing out here among the trees? The gringos seemed like ghosts that only appeared through the mouths of Ramiro Ramirez and Clemente Furia Jr. "The big boss says that we're going too slow, he says this, he tells us to do that." It had been three days and I hadn't seen hide nor hair of a *gringo*.

I only had seen the contractor, Ramiro Ramirez. Once in a while he comes around to keep an eye on us. He exchanges a few words with Clemente Furia Jr., in English and in his border Spanglish, then he takes off. I think Ramiro Ramirez is as Mexican as a prickly pear. Despite the fact that you can tell that he's just pretending that he doesn't speak Spanish all that well. He says goodbye with a few words in English and then ends up in Spanish with Clemente Furia Jr., who can speak a little *gringo*.

I wish that these were my grandparents' orchards. I would be running around catching butterflies, looking for weeds for my rabbits to eat and gathering firewood to heat up tortillas. If this were my grandfather's land, right now we would be harvesting honey from the honeycombs. Honey as transparent as drops of water, with the scent of orange and lime blossoms.

Why am I here in the lands of *Aztlán*? What am I looking for? Why did I come here to this country? Cholver and Cuerna have been here for years and years and they are still stuck to this land that pulls us like a magnet. Some of the guys offer to pay their way back just because they know that those two would never take them up on it.

"Cholver, I'll pick up the tab for your ticket to Mexico."

"No way! Don't fuck around. I'm not going, not in a million years. Not even if you gave me the money to go on a plane. I'm not going, and that's that."

"You're going to die an old man here."

"What the hell do you care?"

Cholver and Cuerna are stuck here in this land as if it belonged to them. Their faces are furrowed and dark like the earth. Lying down on the ground they blend in like camouflage, and their skin looks like an earthen leather stretched across their cheekbones. Maybe this earth does belong to them. Or maybe it always has belonged to them. I imagine that this land is like en enormous magnet that calls to the iron in our blood, in our Mexican blood. The wrinkled skin of the oldest workers is a living camouflage against this earth of *Aztlán*.

These orchards are very green, flowering, and very clean, but they seem sad to me. You don't hear the roosters crow or the church bells ring. At night I don't hear the crickets sing and I haven't seen the thick darkness of the bats. Neither have I seen anybody working the land with their team of oxen or with a pair of mules. Only huge yellow machines kicking up clouds of dust as they dig furrows. Just seeing them makes me cough. Sometimes I wonder: are those machines leaving the earth thinned out, like we leave the peach trees? I ask myself, where are the people that pasture the flocks? Where are the old men who go by and wave their hat in greeting as they pass you in the road? Where are the ladies that flap their shawls when they see someone working the land with the sweat of his brow?

I don't know why the bosses or Clemente Furia Jr. don't lend us money to buy food. Today we already have worked twelve hours. In three days we have worked thirty-six hours snipping off little hard green balls. Today was just like yesterday. The boss left us at the Ranch House and drove off. There's no hope of eating today, or tomorrow for that matter.

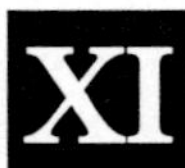

Green Peach Fritters

Little Clown was the only one who took a shower. He put on the same shirt he was wearing yesterday. He only has two changes of clothes. I saw him walk back into the August Ladies and I thought he had gone to masturbate. The recent arrivals, the first thing they look for is their own private spot in the orchard.

Little Clown came back with a big pile of little green peaches wrapped up in his shirt. He washed them, split them in half, and took out the seeds. He turned on the stove with the pliers and put them to fry with a little lard that he found in the cabinet. It had never occurred to anybody to cook the green peaches, so many of which go to waste on the ground. That night we ate a feast of peach fritters. The next two days we ate them boiled, but by the third day nobody wanted any more because we all got hit with a diarrhea from hell. Everybody blamed Chapo and Parrot for not washing their hands before cutting them up and putting them on to boil.

We all just can't wait for Saturdays because it's the day we find out how much we owe the company after a week of working.[3] The boss takes us to a grocery store called Wetbacks' Market, owned by some gringos,

---

3 In the original Spanish, "el Día de la Raya," literally the day of the slash. In the peonage system, not distinctively different from the informal agricultural sector portrayed here, all of the workers' expenditures of the week (accommodations, food, transportation, medicine, etc.) would be noted in a ledger with slash marks, more comprehensible than words to the illiterate workers, small lines that indicated each amount to be subtracted from the wages. Often, a meager subsistence provided by the Company left the workers owing money by payday, so that they stayed in continual debt.

that's just outside of town. He gave us the bad news that the company hadn't cut us checks because we all were in the red, but he said that we could pick up anything we wanted at the store on credit. We jumped out of the van like greased pigs coming out of the pen. At the Wetbacks' Market there were three blonde girls as cashiers and two big old white boys in charge of cashing checks and serving the plates of chicken or pork chops by the pound or the awful tamales that were kept warm under a light bulb.

The store's owner and Clemente Furia Jr. finished talking and gave us the green light. The little blonde gals stared at us with a blank expression on their faces, punctuated with the well-known "Oh my God!" Down the aisles we walked, leaving behind us a trail of dirt and in the cool air conditioning who knows what stench, because the big-butted blondes just wrinkled their noses.

Clemente Furia Jr. ordered us roasted chickens, corn tortillas, jalapeño peppers, soft drinks, and a few twenty-four-packs of beer. Underneath a tree that was on the side of the store we sat down to eat. We laid out the chicken on the plastic bags and Kalimán, who already had opened up the can of jalapeño peppers with this knife, dumped them out. Nobody remembered to wash their hands, and we plunged into the banquet like a pack of starving dogs.

That night there was a drunken party at the Ranch House. Everybody drank except for Little Clown and Old Andrade. At eight o'clock at night I had drunk a six-pack by the time Clemente Furia Jr. showed up with some friends. They came to sell us marijuana and cocaine. He passed two packets over to Chicho. One small one with snow and the other bulkier one with weed.

""How much did you sell him?" I asked Furia. "If you have any crack, I'll buy some. Fucking weed and dust don't work so well for me."

"Look here, you little jerk-off Monk," said Furia, "If you don't like it, asshole, then fuck your mother. What do you mean, how much did I sell *him*? Don't be thinking you're not part of all of this, because here it's everybody to hell or everybody to heaven, and not like your damned racist religion. Here you all pay for the dope and the coke. The bastard who doesn't want any can get the hell out and look for work someplace else."

I stopped sharpening the blade of my knife and put it back in its sheath. I stood up as I lit a cigarette and I walked out of the yard and toward the bridge.

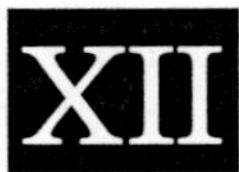

Gonorrhea

In the wintertime, it would already be dark before we left off pruning, even though it was barely five or five-thirty at night. In the tiny cobbled-together shower, Little Clown, his blood still warmed from going at it with the shears, because he had been pruning all damned day, ducks under the faucet of ice-cold water. Between gritted teeth he chomps on the furious water that falls like needles onto his fourteen year-old manhood. The water feels like it penetrates to his very bones, like the pruned branches stab into the frozen earth.

Behind one of the Ranch House's glassless windows, Little Clown and Old Andrade were blessed with the vision of Selma's generous white buttocks. The girl was trying to hide among the plants in the garden to pee. Three carnivorous ferns were sleeping beneath the shadow of the big ash trees, but the ferns unfurled immediately at the touch of Selma's great buttocks. A mist of fresh urine seemed to flower over the green moss in the garden of trees at the Ranch House.

From the bare window jamb, with cigarette smoke clouding around his eyes, Old Andrade gently recounted how he bathed every day at four o'clock in the morning just to avoid the urge to masturbate to the image of Selma in the nude.

Boss Clemente was coming to get us at five-thirty in the morning to go and prune in the vineyards and peach and cherry orchards. In his little truck we would all ride along like matches nestled in a box. Our pestilent morning breath would steam up the polarized panes of the truck.

Arriving at the orchard, Clemente Furia would assign each worker to a line of trees. The first tree in each row had a sign with a name that wasn't the name of the worker.

"Ramplas, you're going to be Gilberto Torres. You, Chicho, are going to be Jaime Cervantes, and Little Clown, you're going to be..." Little Clown didn't let the Boss finish his sentence and told him that he wanted to work under his grandfather's name.

Clemente Furia Jr. asked him for his social security card. Little Clown took out of his pants' pocket a worn blue card. You could barely make out the nine numbers of his grandfather's social security card.

"You probably picked up this piece of shit in the flea market. I don't want any fucking made-up social security numbers," Clemente Furia Jr. yelled, furiously ripping the card out of the boy's hand and directing his words to everyone so that the entire squadron would hear his verdict.

Clemente Furia Jr. hung a sign with the name of Daniel Campos on Little Clown's tree. Everybody kept their mouth shut, like usual. For years nobody had dared to disobey Clemente Furia Jr.'s orders, and they wouldn't until I started to stir up the henhouse by getting social security cards and amnesty papers for the farm workers, since the news was saying that President Ronald Reagan would sign off on them.

"Tree, little tree, fucking tree, I'm gonna leave you smooth like a baby's butt," Chapo grunted as he slid a pair of green socks onto his hands to protect them from the cold, and between gritted teeth he sobbed with rage at the sight of a cherry tree that looked more like a mesquite it was so big.

We sharpened the pruning shears and started to clip the cherry tree's beards until they were nice and neat. Every day for three months, until five or six at night you could hear the snapping of the branches among the steel leaves of the shears. We always had nicely greased armpits from the sweat, not to mention our asses.

The boss went over to Selma and started chatting her up. Then he asked her who she had slept with the night before.

"You think that I'm some cheap slut, or what," Selma answered him, irritated.

"Don't tell me you haven't fucked Old Andrade, he may be old, but I bet he's hung like a horse," the boss growled with a sarcastic chuckle.

Selma, her eyes bright with rage, kept on pruning her tree without saying a word. The boss, puffing on a joint, walked over to Old Andrade and asked after Pinto.

"Why didn't he get up to work? Did he get shit-faced last night?"

"No. He hasn't been drinking for more than a month."

"So?"

The boss went on all day long about how he was going to dock Pinto two days for missing work without notice. Saturday afternoon, Furia talked to Pinto. Pinto had to pay him the twenty-five dollars for transportation and the twelve bucks for the week's sodas without having drunk them.

In the afternoon, after we got out of work, Pinto really didn't talk with anyone. He just sat on the dried-up tree trunk outside of the house and by himself he would smoke his dope. You could see the sadness in the depths of his eyes.

The next day, Pinto didn't show up at work again and Clemente Furia Jr. fired him for not wanting to pay for transport and soft drinks and for refusing to tell him why he was missing work. A week later we found out that he had gone to an appointment he had at a clinic. That's when the boss told Old Andrade that the spots on Pinto's skin were past curing, that he was wasting his time seeing the doctor.

"Well, I don't know. All he told me was that he had gone to the doctor to see about those spots that he had," Andrade said.

Clemente Furia Jr. shouted so that everybody heard.

"Better hope those spots on his skin aren't like the gonorrhea that Chicho and Chapo have on their dicks. You better run on over to the clinic tomorrow, huh Chicho?"

"Yeah, well. That fat chick gave us gonorrhea right on the head of our cocks, both me and Chapo. And just because we didn't put on a rain coat. But I'm so pissed off that the next time that gal comes this way, I'm gonna kick her ever-lovin' ass."

"Oh, so it's her fault, Chicho?" Selma asked, angry.

"Don't take me all serious, Selma, I'm just talkin'. You get mad at everything. Next time she comes around, I'm gonna wear a rubber sack, even if it feels like hell."

The boss wanted to scare Chapo and Chicho so he told them that they'd have to get a shot of penicillin in their penis to cure the infection. He told them that they were going to do it with a needle the size of a maguey cactus spine. Then he said that the doctor might have to cut off their dicks. They had tied one on they were so scared, but they sobered up real quick when in the clinic parking lot the Border Patrol showed up with patrol cars, dogs, and a mini-plane up in the sky. From the clinic the dog trucks filled up with pregnant women, teenagers, kids, and old men. That night, in a cell in Fresno County, Chapo writhed around on the floor as if he needed to go to the bathroom. Tears of pus were weeping from his dick. A man who was sitting on the floor held his wife's hand tightly and told Chapo in a sympathetic voice to be strong, to not be a faggot. But big fat drops of pain leaked out of Chapo's eyes. The man was telling him, although Chapo wasn't even listening, that his two twelve year-old girls had been left alone in the house.

"You don't even have a wife, or children. Tomorrow you can come back across and no big deal. Don't be a crybaby, pal."

There in the cell stories flew about how the Border Patrol had caught them.

"They got me like Saint Julia's tiger.[4] I walked into the Four of Clubs to take a dump and the bastards came in and grabbed me. They didn't even give me time to wipe my ass."

Others talked about how they planned to get back to *Aztlán*. Some planned to go on south and to cultivate their own piece of land, plant pintos, garbanzos, and corn, even if it was sharecropping. Others were going to try to cross back as soon as they had eaten a few chicken necks and gizzards in Tijuana.

"Ay, Tijuana, Tijuanita, I'm gonna see you again!" shouted one of the workers, in tears, as the bus took off toward the south.

---

4 The legendary story of José de Jesús Negrete Medina, retold in a Mexican film by Alejandro Gamboa (2002) is of a Robin Hood type who was caught by the authorities with his pants down, relieving himself.

The next day, at eight o'clock in the morning, the bus stopped in front of a barbed-wire fence. The Border Patrol officials opened two doors, one on the bus and the other a gate that opened into Mexicali. The agents put in earplugs so they didn't have to listen to the swear words that the undocumented aliens were yelling at them as they climbed down out of the van. The deported were cussing everybody and their momma as they stepped onto Mexican soil. The agents pretended like they didn't understand and said goodbye, smiling through clenched teeth.

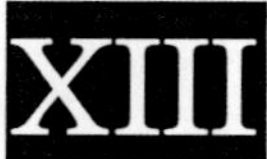

Tijuana

"Come on in, come on in, young man, to the best restaurant in Tijuana. Here in Kentucky Fried Gizzards we have the best appetizers in all of Baja." A young man, wearing an apron blackened with grime, talked up the store and with a square of cardboard shooed away the flies that landed on the gizzards and necks of fried chicken.

"Come on in, come on in. Here the *coyote* takes his little chicks, and the whole darn henhouse if that's what you want. He'll take you door to door and for a good price. Califas, Chicago, Las Vegas, Washington, or wherever you want to open up a new border," the young man discreetly approached the table to hawk the *coyotes'* services. "Tonight they're leaving for Chicago and New York. If you want to go to California, go to the front of the Red Windmill and ask for Chita. That bastard is one of the best *coyotes* there are in Tijuana."

The *coyote* Chita had heard the scoop that there was a roadblock in San Clemente. Chita pulled over off of Highway 5 and told his chicks to get out of the truck. Six or seven miles before the road block, Chita sent them running through the hills.

"I'll be waiting for you three or four miles past the road block. You've got more or less an hour to get there. Who ever gets there gets there, and whoever doesn't is fucked. And I'm not waiting any longer than an hour. Everybody follow Doll and do whatever he says."

In the darkness of night they started running as far away from the highway as possible. Everything was run, run, run to get where Chita, the *coyote* was waiting.

Among the stones they tripped, they got back up, they pushed, they were stabbed by stickers, they cursed, but they kept on running hopefully toward the north.

"I'm telling you to get down, you bastards! Don't you hear the helicopter?" From the brush and the darkness, Doll, Chita's helper, yelled at them, infuriated. "The *Migra* is getting close. You, you old bitch, pull in your gut. You look like a water jug."

"I can't suck it in any more," responded with panic a rotund lady. "How do you expect me to pull it in if I can't hide it any better than this?"

The Border Patrol agents found the squadron of undocumented aliens there in the bushes. The whole bunch dispersed in the darkness, except for the fat woman who stayed in her hiding place, stuck like a jack-knifed eighteen-wheeler. The woman got up from her burrow and seeing herself outfoxed, she threw her arms around a big stocky agent.

"Ay, mister, don't deport me back to my country. You don't look like a bad man; you're not mean like the other guys, are you? Just look at your big, strong arms. Ay, what a pretty white boy you are! Just look at those deep blue eyes of yours! You are so handsome! Just let me go on my way. I'm not going to hurt anyone. I just want to find a life here in your country. Come on, now! Don't be mean, please."

The agent, without knowing what to do, extricated himself from the lady's arms and retreated, leaving her alone in the darkness.

On the other side of the roadblock in San Clemente, Chita was waiting for his cargo. His helper brought him up to date about what happened, and he had to wait longer than he had planned. He waited almost until dawn, when through the light of the rising sun he could make out the fat lady who was approaching, out of breath but bravely forging on.

Chita the *coyote* crossed the border once, twice, three, four or five times a week. In reality, the physical border didn't exist for him. Sometimes he went through legally with his green card and other times he came through the hills with his chicks. Chita came and went between the two countries. He would sleep in one and wake up in the other. He would drink a beer in Tijuana and piss it out in San Diego.

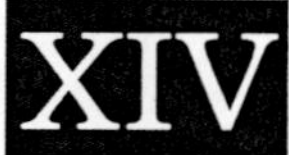

Old Andrade

Fresh meat, fresh meat," dropping his barbells on the old hardwood floor, Chapo yelled, talking about the two prostitutes who were walking through the back door of the Ranch House.

One was tall, her skin tanned golden brown, and she charged twenty dollars. The other one was blonde, fat, and she charged ten or fifteen, sliding scale. Just about every Saturday night those two prostitutes would come, all the way from Fresno, here to the Ranch House, which is on the outskirts of Reedley, California. I don't know how the two whores found us here, since the Ranch House is hidden among miles of orchards.

"Chapo, lend me ten bucks. I'll pay you back next Saturday." Prudencio Armenta slowly and deeply breathed in the smoke from his joint as he asked Chapo.

In one corner of the living room there was a card game going on between Melquiades, Lefty, Chicho, and two workers who had arrived a week before to work the pruning season. The card game stopped when the two prostitutes walked in. They pulled their skirts up, shucked off their panties, and tossed them in among the cards.

Somebody said to clear out the main room of the Ranch House. Six workers who were drinking beer and watching porn flicks came out of the big room. In the entire filthy and cold house, that was the only room that had a cot for a bed, a door, and a window.

Selma, a worker barely twenty-two years old, walked off into the kitchen to make herself some coffee. Selma had come to the Ranch House a month ago and she hadn't worked off even a third of what she owed Boss Clemente Furia Jr. on account of food, rent, dope, and transportation. To the eight hundred dollars noted down in his book, Furia had added eighty-five dollars for a pair of second-hand pruning shears.

The skinny prostitute came over to Little Clown and put her ass right on his head of straight hair. Little Clown got up and stuck into the middle of a notebook a sheet of paper, where he had just started writing a letter that said:

December 12, 1985

Dear Virgin Mary,

I hope that my letter finds you wrapped in happiness and fortune in your church at the Guadalupe Ranch and your Basilica at Tepeyac too. After sending my greetings, I wanted to say the following: First, I would like to know why you never answered my first two letters. I'm sure that I put enough stamps on them. Is it that the parish priest at the Basilica didn't give them to you? In the first letter I sent you a twenty-dollar bill. I don't know if maybe you were expecting me to send more and so you are offended, it's just that here in the pruning season it's like a kick in the pants, that is to say, it's not going so great for any of us farm workers. We barely earn enough to eat scraps.

In my second letter I sent you twenty-five dollars and you haven't answered that one either, not even to let me know you got the money. In this letter I'm not sending you anything because things are really hard around here. Anyway, I think that these days you're getting more than enough offerings.

Look, some guests just arrived at the Ranch House. I better write more later, when I can finish telling you what my friend Mateo thinks about you, about the saints, eternal life, and God.

P.S. My friend Mateo is the one who taught me to read and write.

Little Clown closed the notebook where he was writing and scurried out of the Ranch House. Outside, Old Andrade was by himself like usual, close to a campfire warming his sixty-six year-old arthritic bones. Little

Clown, without looking at Old Andrade, quietly made his way over to the fire. Out of the corner of his eyes he would glance over at how Old Andrade smoked his Marlboro.

"So, you little shit, aren't you going to fuck? Don't tell me you don't like whoring around like this whole gang of son of a bitch dope fiends here." Old Andrade questioned Little Clown, watching him as he threw his empty cigarette pack onto the fire.

Without saying a word, Little Clown shook his head no. Andrade stared at him with a look that conveyed his many years of experience.

"You done good, you son of a bitch," he said in a quiet voice, as he held out his trembling hands toward the fire.

The light of the lantern, the only one that there was at the Ranch House, shone its honey-colored light through the dirty windowpane. A bird with an injured wing tried to get close to the warmth of the honey light of the lantern. Inside the Ranch House you could hear noises and fumbling around that made the bird anxious. The flames of the campfire sometimes would turn yellow, blue, or red. It all depended on the color of the empty cans or the color of the label on the plastic or glass bottles thrown onto the fire.

Prudencio Armenta, Chicho, Chapo, and three other workers came over to the campfire, rolling joints, smug satisfied smiles on their faces. Prudencio Armenta told Little Clown that it was his turn with one of the whores. Scared witless, he responded saying he didn't have any money.

"Chapo will lend you the dough," Armenta sneered at him.

"You want me to lend you some money, bud?" Chapo asked him, sticking his hand into his pocket and grabbing his wallet.

"This little son of a bitch Little Bird or Little Clown or whatever already owes me a hundred bucks for all the times he gives it to the whore who work out of the motel in town," Andrade chimed in quickly, getting Little Clown out of the jam. Everybody started to laugh.

"Damn buddy, you sure play your cards close to your chest!"

Little Clown didn't say anything, but he looked proud. He sat there wondering if he really did owe the hundred bucks to Old Andrade. It was true that Andrade would lend the other workers money and charge them incredibly high interest, but he couldn't owe him anything because he had never borrowed from anybody. Old Andrade must have made a mistake, because he was so old, or maybe it was one of his little jokes that he always was making.

Old Andrade loved to play jokes on the other workers. One time he pulled a good one on the bunch of card players. Old Andrade came in shouting and asking whose fifty dollars it was that had fallen in the kitchen corner. Lefty got up right away off the floor and saying it was his. Old Andrade asked him if he was sure that the money was his. Lefty pulled his wallet out of his pocket and showed him that indeed he was missing fifty bucks.

"Well, you better hurry up, because the Devil is going to grab it right out of your hands," replied Andrade with a straight face.

Lefty ran to the kitchen and everybody ran behind him. When they got to the kitchen nobody could see the fifty dollars. There was a moment of silence, and Andrade pointed with one finger at a dirty, fly-covered rag in one of the corners of the kitchen. Lefty ran, picked up the rag, and everybody busted a gut laughing because what was underneath the rag was a human turd.

Little Clown continued to ponder about the money that supposedly Andrade had lent him. He thought it must be a bad joke that he was trying to play on him. Nonetheless he didn't dare ask him when he had lent him the money. Mockingly, Chapo pretended to figure out the interest for the hundred dollar debt that Little Clown was supposed to pay Old Andrade. El Chapo figured out that he already would owe twenty bucks in interest for the week. Old Andrade corrected him, saying that the sum of the interest was already forty bucks, because he had lent him the money two weeks ago. Little Clown kept his mouth shut and didn't say a word.

Pedro Cantu drifted over to the campfire with a beer in one hand and asked if anybody wanted one. The workers all went off to drink, except for Old Andrade and Little Clown. When Cantu saw that Little Clown wasn't going to drink, he ordered him harshly to accept a beer.

"Go to hell, Cantu. He doesn't drink. Do you think that he's a drunk just like the rest of you?" Andrade scolded Cantu.

Little Clown felt Old Andrade was in his corner. Cantu mad a face like he didn't care and dedicated himself to his beer. For a minute Old Andrade and Little Clown stayed silent beside the campfire.

"Hey, little shit, it's not true that you're broke, is it?"

Little Clown just shook his head to say no.

"Son of a bitch, so what do you do with the money that you earn?" asked Old Andrade, shocked.

"I send it to my mother in Mexico," Little Clown told him softly.

"You done good, you son of a bitch. Don't be like these crappy dope fiends. Just look at them, they spend every penny on whores and then end up asking to borrow money from me so they have something to put in their stomach during the week. They're going to hell. I charge them interest and if they like it, fine, if not, eat shit."

The honey light from the lantern was fading little by little through the dense winter fog. The injured wing of the bird looked more and more like the slanted roof of the Ranch House bathroom.

"Save your money, while you're still young. Look at me. Because I was fooling around like this idiot bunch here, I don't have anything put away. Now I'm an old man and I can barely work. I can't stop working because I don't have papers so I can't retire. I have worked all my life in this fucking shitty valley and what has it got me? When I got here in 1968, I was the one who planted Santa Rosa trees in this very orchard. I was the one who burned the fields, and I was the one who planted King of Diamonds, Elegant Ladies. Look, seven years ago we planted this orchard of August Ladies. It hurts me right here in my chest because I know that I won't ever again see them throw out buds and flower so pretty, like they do every March," weepy-eyed, remembered Andrade.

Little Clown turned to look Old Andrade right in the eye. His eyes of centuries, set in that face of leather molded of clay, took on a brilliance with the wetness of his tears. Old Andrade, with heavy steps of a hard winter, turned toward the door to the Ranch House basement. Little Clown stayed watching the bird with the fallen wing. Over the campfire, wounded by the night chill, drops of mist bathed in blood drifted down from the lantern. Little Clown caught up with Old Andrade and held out his hand to help him down the steps of the Ranch House. When he got down to the basement, Old Andrade's entire body dropped like a fallen wing. It was as if the earth had reclaimed him. Old Andrade, who had talked so lovingly to the earth, now was there with her to rest his eternal exhaustion of a farm worker. Little Clown laid him out on the cold shadowy ground, crossed his arms over his chest, and closed his eyelids. May he rest in peace, Old Andrade, who was buried and mourned in the oblivion of the Ranch House cellar.

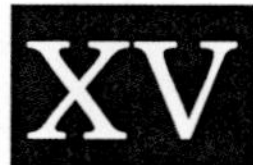

Clemente Furia Senior

You son of a whore! How many times do I have to tell you to not be giving me any food cooked with garlic! I hate fucking garlic," complained Clemente Furia Jr. to Maria, incensed...

Clemente Furia Sr. ordered them to finish picking the rest of the garlic and to start putting some muscle into it. The workers, sweaty and stinking, carried the sacks and piled them into the truck. Young Clemente's feet stumbled from the weight of the bags, but his father straightened them out with his belt.

Clemente Furia Jr., sitting at the table but not eating, thought back to that afternoon when his father pulled him out of grade school to take him to pick garlic. Since then young Clemente couldn't get the stench of his misfortune out of his head.

Young Clemente, at ten years old, had fallen deeply in love with Alma. They didn't give him any time to tell her how much he loved her. That day, that very day when his father went for him at the school, he had decided to declare his love to Almita, Almita.

"You have to go. Get your things and walk on out that way because your father has come to get you," the teacher said to young Clemente.

* * *

"Get a move on, you old son of a bitch! Move those hands!" Clemente Furia Jr., now foreman of the Ranch House, shouted at his father.

"I'm already busting my balls, you son of a bitch. Look, you can't even see my hands with the flurry of these pecker peaches, White Ladies."

"Shut the hell up and move it like you were last night. That's what you got to do!"

"Son of a bitch, that's easy for you to say, you're not wearing this pack. I'd like to se you try to carry it. I've seventy-something years old and look, you and your gang of dope fiends there, I kick your ass and you come back to have me kick it again. You're not to old for me to give you a good licking, you sons of bitches!"

"Shut up you fucking old fart."

"You shut up, son of a bitch."

"Son of a bitch or son of a whore?"

"Clemente, don't start with that again."

"It's not my fault that your old lady was a whore."

"Look, Clemente, don't be talking that way about your momma."

"About my momma or about your old lady?"

"Don't be an asshole, man. The Virgin is going to punish you."

"Fuck their mothers, both of them, the whores."

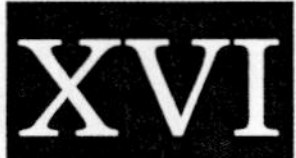

Purificación del Refugio

For the last two years Gil had been saving every extra dollar because he was engaged to Purificación del Refugio. In the two years that Gil had lived at the Ranch House nobody saw him go with a single prostitute. Some of the guys thought that maybe Gil liked men. What was for sure was that Gil was very faithful to his fiancée, who he had proposed to and left behind in the village of Purísima, Guanajuato.

Two months before the wedding day, Gil's buttocks started drying out and he had lost around 30 pounds. You could see exhaustion in his face and his footsteps. One Saturday Gil was looking especially pale, and not even the weekly check could motivate him. The guys gathered around, giving him little slaps on the back to cheer him up. Clement Furia Jr. advised him that what he needed was a good fuck and to smoke a joint to get his spirits up. Chicho and Chapo said that Gil was feeling weak because he was such a louse. Gil would perk up a little whenever he would get a letter from Purificación del Refugio. In her letters she would chat about all the wedding preparations and how happy her mother was, who would be Gil's mother-in-law.

"My Purificación's wedding will be one of the best of the year," Doña Rosa would boast to her friends. "My future son-in-law is from the North, and Teodula, the gal who brings the mail, says that he's always sending registered letters with nice fat money orders from the U.S."

The wedding preparations were going along swimmingly. But of course Gil wasn't able to attend the obligatory preparatory sessions at the Church. So the fiancées were not going to be able to marry if they couldn't figure out how to comply with the Church's requirements. Don Petronilo solved the problem with a large bill and a little pig. Manuel, one of Gil's first cousins, would stand in for Gil at the sessions.

The pigs, chickens, turkeys and goats were fat, dumb and happy in the corral. Gil's mother Doña Jacinta already had the stock pots, chili peppers, rice, and all the necessary condiments to make enough mole so that the guests couldn't gossip about her like that other time.

Purificación del Refugio was stunned every time they tore off another page from the calendar. She imagined that before she knew it she would be in her boyfriend's arms. After the New Year, Gil would take her up to the United States. Purificación del Refugio was worried that she would start her period on her wedding day. She prayed to the sainted Virgin to grant her the miracle of sending her period early in the month of December. Purificación wanted to smell like flowers on the day she married. The Avon lady took advantage to sell her all kinds of stuff for "feminine hygiene." Her mother had to sell a piglet to pay the bill for all the special ointments and creams that were necessary for newlyweds.

At night Purificación del Refugio laid awake imagining herself dressed in white, beside her fiancée Gil. Then suddenly she would be all in a tizzy and for the life of her couldn't get a wink of sleep because she felt embarrassed. She felt embarrassed because in the church all of the people from the whole town would be watching her. That night her husband would make mad, passionate love to her. She felt embarrassed to think that a bunch of boys from the village would gather in the street outside their house to listen for her cries of pain as she lost her virginity. All sorts of thoughts came in to her head and before she knew it she would be naked in her bed. There on top of the covers she would spread her legs, run her hands over her breasts, and move her had down to squeeze her sex. She wanted to touch herself tenderly where her flesh was warm, but she didn't dare for fear of losing her chastity.

Gil arrived in Purísima on December 8th. He got there just in time to show up at the office of the Civil Registry in Purísima. Gil looked wiped out, but nobody noticed because he perked right up with all of the wedding preparations. It was the most anticipated wedding of the year in all of Purísima.

After every civil ceremony in Purísima, the townspeople would eat their fill of soups and turkey mole. But for the first time in many years there was no soup and no turkey mole in Purísima. Most of the children had to content themselves with beans and most of the men didn't get to eat anything, because the wives hadn't made dinner that day that the judge at the Civil Registry refused to marry the bride and groom.

The office of the Civil Registry was where the scandal began, because the judge announced that he couldn't marry the couple under these circumstances. Throughout Purísima the word was spread that Purificación del Refugio and Gil couldn't get married, but nobody knew why. The judge didn't want to say anything publicly and had the couple and their families brought into an inner chamber. All over town they started speculating that maybe Purificación del Refugio and Gil were too closely related to marry. Others said that the judge, Don Cipriano, had liked Purificación del Refugio for more than three years, since before she was engaged to Gil, and that maybe he was coming up with some excuse not to marry them. The women gossiped that Purificación del Refugio had lost her virginity with Fausto Martínez. Everybody knew that at one time she had been Fausto's girlfriend. People had plenty to say about the bride, but nobody would have imagined that Gil had turned up positive for HIV on his blood tests.

"But Your Honor, that is a decision that the bride should make, not the law," complained Doña Rosa angrily. "Who are you to make decisions for my daughter, who is in love?"

"I am sorry to have to tell you that the HIV virus is an infectious illness that can be fatal," explained the judge with eloquence. "Young Gil Uribe could infect Purificación del Refugio, and she could pass the illness on to her children before they were even born. You see, before becoming a judge, I studied a semester in the medical school in our capital, Guanajuato."

"But what in the hell kind of idiocy is this illness, after all?" asked Gil's father. "After all, we all are going to die sooner or later. So what's the big deal? And according to you, ain't nobody can't get married on account of this ridiculous disease."

Don Cipriano ended the private meeting. Don Catarino already had run around to all of the cooks and the guests that were to be at his house, but then somebody suggested that he announce over the loudspeaker that everybody come to his house to eat, but nobody showed up. The enormous pots of soup and turkey mole got wormy, the pork casseroles and barbecued goat spoiled on the patio, because the whole town found out about the infectious disease that Gil had brought from the United States, and they were afraid of getting close to the Uribe house. Gil shut himself up in his room and for hours didn't even want to come out to go to the bathroom for fear of infecting his bride. The next morning, the cattle herders and shepherds avoided passing close to the Uribe house because they were afraid that the animals would get sick.

Purificación del Refugio was not resigned to losing her fiancée forever. There she stayed, next to the door to Gil's room, like a faithful puppy. She begged him between sobs to open the door and to come out and eat, or at least drink some water. Doña Rosa came looking for her daughter at the Uribes', and seeing her close to the room where Gil was, walked up and threw handfuls of lime at her so that she wouldn't get infected with HIV.

Gil lasted three days without eating or drinking anything, until a medical researcher from the United States showed up. Dr. Smith, together with his two assistants, set themselves up in the Uribe house. The people of Purísima were shocked that the gringos weren't afraid of getting infected. Stunned, the folks watched from a distance as the young doctor and his helpers took Gil's pulse and peered into his mouth.

Dr. Smith started Gil on a treatment regime, because he had gotten quite weak on account of his three-day fast and the HIV. Gil seemed a little better after three days, and Dr. Smith was able to have a long conversation with him. One afternoon, Dr. Smith convinced his patient to ride with him on horseback through the fields of the town.

For a month the wheat and barley fields had started to populate the black earth of Purísima with shafts of green. The fields and plains gave Gil back his voice. Dr. Smith and his assistants spoke perfect Spanish, so it wasn't hard for them to carry out their research on AIDS and HIV.

XVII

Jinx

Don't let it get away! Don't let it escape! Don't let that goddamned son of a bitch lizard escape!"

"Grab it, you damned Jinx!"

"Jinx, did you let it get away?"

"That's just my luck…"

* * *

One winter day Scarface found a lizard nest in the basement of the dilapidated Ranch House. In a nest made of straw and trash were hibernating three generations of lizards, rolled up into each other and camouflaged with the dark and dusty earth untouched for years by the sun. By the size of the creatures you could tell that in the same nest there were grandparents, parents, and a new litter of four babies.

Scarface called his buddies over. Like starving savages Chicho and Chapo crept up to the nest of reptiles and grabbed the two biggest lizards by the head. Three other guys took care of the little ones.

They placed the innocent lizards on top of an Elegant Lady trunk and one by one cut their heads off with a single swipe, before the little things could make a peep. All of them got the same treatment, death by machete, except for one of the littlest ones, who skittered off through the weeds, saving himself from the butchery practiced by the Ranch House workers.

"Grab it, Jinx! Don't let it get away!"

"Did you catch it?"

"No, I don't know where it's got to… That's just my luck…"

The workers chopped up the lizards and put them on to boil in a soup pot. That afternoon, the workers under foreman Clement Furia Jr. dined on a lizard soup without any more seasoning than salt and a handful of wild parsley. The lizard soup took on a muddy color like water from washing dirty socks, but it felt like heaven to the wrinkled stomachs of the field workers. That same day the Ranch House hands finished the last of the soup and fell back to take a nap in their beds of cardboard, grease still covering their lips and a bitter taste of hell on their tongues.

Jinx, as he dozed, felt a tickle in his pants pocket. It was the baby lizard that had managed to survive, thanks to Jinx, who had pretended he got away. The lizard stuck his head up and began to explore the Ranch House. He climbed down Crip's legs, up Pachuco's cot, over the Mute's head and Kalimán's chest, ending up hopping from belly to belly. They were bellies temporarily swelled by the nutritious broth. It almost seemed as if the little creature could tell that his family was within the workers' tummies, because as he twirled about like a top he scratched their belly buttons. In fact, of course, his ancestors were there inside those halfway-inflated human balloons, but by that time they already were being absorbed by the piranha-like digestive systems inside the starving field hands.

* * *

Lively, which was the name that Jinx gave the surviving lizard, turned into the mascot of the Ranch House workers. He made it through the pruning season, feeding himself on weeds, insects, unripe fruit, and from time to time a strip of tortilla that Jinx would toss him in bed. Jinx carried him around to work in the field. As he was pruning trees on an 18-foot ladder, he would let Lively hunt for bugs on the branches of the Santa Rosas, King of Diamonds, White Ladies, Elegant Ladies, or August Ladies. Little Clown would perch him on his shoulders. The Mute would pat his head and talk sweetly to him like a human mother talks to her baby. Kalimán would scratch his belly, and the damned lizard would stretch out on the ground with his feet up in the air, playing dead. Chicho would blow clouds of marijuana smoke at him, and Lively, with his melancholy face, just blinked his little eyes.

"Look, Jinx, I've got the beggar stoned to the gills."

During the fruit harvest Lively had a good time of it in the Ranch House, with the abundance of fruit, insects, and corn tortillas. That summer, Lively grew more than six inches. Summer is when there is plenty of work in the San Joaquin Valley in California, and it's when at the Ranch House there are a wealth of whores, beer, and drugs. On several occasions they got Lively to try beer and coke. Lively grew happy and hearty within the human habitat of the field hands. The workers spoiled him, but some merely wanted to see him on their plate.

"Beggar, you cute darling, just look how big you are getting. You're just about right for a nice stew…"

During the winter in the San Joaquin Valley not only isn't there enough work; on top of that, the cold becomes increasingly cruel. There wasn't heat or hot water at the Ranch House. The workers slept in their work clothes and sometimes even with their shoes on. Jinx nestled Lively in a corner of a room and made him a nest there. Lively survived one winter, two winters in the Ranch House. When he was two years old, he was already more that two feet long and weighed more than eight pounds. In one day he would eat more than three corn tortillas and three raw eggs; he would gobble up a bunch of grapes before you could blink. Lively learned to eat table food during the good times when work was plenty, but he also lived through months of scarcity, barely subsisting on bread, water, and the odd bug, just like the field hands at the Ranch House during the winter.

Clemente Furia, the foreman, would tell them, "You are some unlucky sons of bitches." He would say that because they weren't able to save even a five dollar bill. A few of them sent their spare change to their families in Mexico, the rest spent all their money on their vices. The winter would come along, and Clemente Furia would promise to lend them money, on credit, to buy food. For one reason or another, Clemente Furia then would disappear from the Ranch House for weeks at a time, and the workers had to figure out some way or another to find something to eat. All of the workers knew that Clemente Furia got the money from their unemployment, and they also knew that he got the money from their tax returns, but nobody dared to say anything to him. They were afraid that they would be run off from the Ranch House, they were afraid of not getting any more work, and they were afraid of being reported to Immigration. Their only recourse was to put up with it. How were they supposed to complain anyway? Who would they complain to, if they didn't even work under their own names? They got checks with somebody else's name and with a social security number that Clemente Furia had found who knew where, but that was valid for claiming unemployment pay and for reporting state and federal taxes. Then Furia would sit back and take all of those benefits that should have gone to the workers. In the meantime, while the field hands suffered cold and hunger, Clemente Furia would be spending all their money in Las Vegas and in clubs along the border.

* * *

Jinx got up early one morning to go hunting. He was hoping to catch a hare over in the King of Diamonds orchard. It was cold as hell. Lively, in the corner of the room, was all curled up into a knot. Jinx walked over to Lively and stroked him along the back and head. Lively just closed his melancholy little eyes.

"Shhh, I'll be right back. I won't be long. I'm going to look for something to eat..."

Jinx covered him up with a blanket that was old, but clean and warm, and went in search of food. Jinx spent the morning looking for anything alive along the shores of a canal. He managed to capture a frog and two hairy rats. When he got back to the Ranch House, he saw his buddies circled around the stove. He smelled the scent of roasted meat and pork rinds. He came up slowly to his friends and they watched him approach like a man burning alive. He dropped the frog and the two rats. They let him through, and he could see Chicho stirring with a wooden spoon the frying meat inside the copper pot. Jinx couldn't believe it. He felt numb inside and out. The fire on the stove flared up, and behind the flames he could see the faces of his friends. More than faces, they looked to him like nameless masks. They were masks with deep gazes, hungry teeth, and sunken mouths. Jinx thought they looked a little like his buddies, like pieces of clay cooking in the fire. Little Clown, Chicho, Chapo, Kalimán, Scarface, Rufas, Coras, the Mute, Pachuco, Parrot. They were all there standing like copper statues. He wanted to remember their names and realized that he couldn't. Better said, nobody ever had actually said their real first names, and what was more, nobody at the Ranch House cared. He tried to recall his own name and felt a lump in his throat.

"Carlos Alberto, which son of a bitch is called Carlos Alberto? I have a letter here for Carlos Alberto," Clemente Furia cracked up laughing. "Ha, ha, ha, it sounds like the name of one of those soap opera characters, Carlos Alberto. Carlos Alberto. They sure stuck it to you when they gave you that name, Jinx. I'll be damned if that doesn't suit you better, Jinx."

How many years had it been since Clemente Furia Jr. had said aloud his first name in the Ranch House? He said it now under his breath, Carlos Alberto, Carlos Alberto. Now his own name sounded strange and even ridiculous to him. So, who was he then? To his buddies he was just Jinx, yes, for them only Jinx existed. His nickname was hopelessly tied to his nature as a good friend, a joker, easy going.

The stockpot over the fire made him think back to a time long ago in Santa Clara del Cobre, in Michoacán, his home town. He must have been about twenty years old, he was wearing a loincloth, he had his hair long, and he had a red bandana tied around his forehead. He was working copper. With an open flame, water, and hammer blows he could transform a sheet of copper into a work of art. The metallic blows still rang out as clearly today as back when he was in the forge with the mallet in his right hand and in his left the polished metal.

The bodies of his friends from the Ranch House looked to him like pieces of copper. The smoke and the fiery smiles of his buddies mixed in with the scents of roasted meat and pork rinds. Inside the stockpot he could see Lively's remains. He backed off without saying a word, and his friends stood there silent. With the wooden spoon, Chicho offered Jinx a morsel of meat from the pot; he turned to see the wordless masks of his friends and decided to take the bite of meat. Jinx brought to his mouth the sizzling piece of fried rind, and you could hear it blister on his tongue like blazing iron in a forge. That's when the rest of the starving workers began to savor with delight the fried skin and roasted meat of the lizard.

Jinx fell to his knees onto the cold earth of the orchard of Santa Rosas, looked toward the sky and cursed:

"Damn this jinx. Damn me, the Jinx."

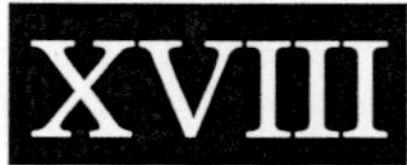

Gil Uribe

I left for the United States two years ago. I assure you that I never have had relations with prostitutes, much less with homosexuals. I swear to you on my manhood, Dr. Smith!"

"And drugs?"

"Well, yes, I've done that. One time I smoked a marijuana cigarette and I also snorted some cocaine. The foreman Clemente Furia Jr. offered it to me and I didn't want to refuse him, because he threatened to fire me. Clemente Furia Jr. wanted me to get addicted so he would have another customer, but I never took marijuana or cocaine from him again. Nevertheless I had to pay for it, whether I did any or not, doctor."

"Tattoos?"

"No, I don't have tattoos on any part of my body."

"Needles?"

"No, Dr. Smith, I never shot up. I never used drugs that you inject into the bloodstream. Look, doctor, I swear by my manhood! As far as I remember, when I was in the Pénjamo Clinic was the only time that I had blood taken. But as you know, that was a requirement imposed by the Civil Registry."

"Fights involving blood?"

"Yes, one time when I was in the sixth grade I got into a fight with one of my classmates. Neither of us got a bloody nose or bled from the mouth. That really got the rest of our classmates riled up with us, because there wasn't much *mole*. *Mole* was another saying that meant blood, doctor."

"I just remembered something, doctor. You know, when I was in my first year of junior high, my friends salted me. It's a game, doctor, to curse somebody. Four of them got me on the ground, held me down by my hands and feet, pulled down my pants and then my underwear. Somebody bared my Johnson, and…"

"Your what?"

"Johnson means dong, doctor, or in other words, my woody."

"What? Please explain what you mean."

"What do you want me to say, doctor? Look, so you understand me, I'm talking about this, my prick, ok?"

"Oh, your penis."

"Penis, peter, dick, or whatever you want to call it. The point is that somebody bared it and then they spit on the very end of it. Before they finished spitting on me they threw a few handfuls of dirt on it. They say that that's how you salt somebody, and curse them to never be able to have children for their whole life. Doctor, the worst of all was when the girls found out that I had been salted. Then they didn't want to be my girlfriend because they believed that I would never be able to get my dong up."

"Your penis."

"Whatever you say, Dr. Smith. I don't want to die, doctor. Just look at the sun. Look at the fields. Why me? Just look how pretty the plains are, doctor. Over here by these banks I liked to come and play with my friends. Look at the river lilies! You can't deny that they're pretty, doctor. The truth is that I don't feel like dying yet, doctor."

"Tell me everything that you are thinking about and exactly how you are feeling."

"I feel like I'm the stubs of the wheat and barley, after the harvest."

"Why?"

"What do you mean, why, doctor? Just wait 'til Conrado, the richest man in Purísima and all the surrounding towns, harvests his crops, then you'll see that it would only take one match to burn down everything that you see in front of you here. Dr. Smith, damned if I don't feel like the wheat chaff. I'd like to go steal one of the matches that Conrado carries around in his pocket. I'd like to strike the match underneath my feet so that my body would burn all night long and the in the morning I could play at whirlwinds with the ashes."

"That's a lovely image."

"I remember that here all along this bank the boys would come to look for *burras*, you know, she-donkeys. They would come with their pockets full of corn on the cob."

"Corn on the cob?"

"Of course, doctor. They would use them to feed to the *burras* while they tried to stick it to them. You should have seen how beautiful that was. They looked like soldiers at the foot of a canyon. In the meanwhile, the pretty girls of Purísima would wear themselves out walking circles around the Plaza. By the time the *burrera* boys showed up to the Plaza the girls had to go home already. Back then I couldn't stop looking at the girls' big butts, but they ignored me and called me a brat. I would get together with other friends my age and bug them throwing orange peels. We would try to hit them right in the middle of their nice big asses, and they would just rub their butts like hot and bothered *burras*. When they found us in the garden trying to torment them, they would get mad and come after us to give us a good thump on the head. When it got dark, the boys and girls my age had to start going home to our houses. The older kids would begin to come down from the banks with their pants pockets empty and smiles like big corncobs. One day I got curious as to what the boys were doing on the banks. I remember that one time I decided to go and find out and I hid behind a *huizache* bush. It was a *huizache* with lots of branches, more or less like this one here. That day I found out that the young men, most of whom were from Northern Mexico, were coming here to fuck the *burras* that were grazing on these plains. Before, all of this was one big plain, but Conrado already had bought it all up. Here all of the animals could eat as much as they wanted, but now, as you can see doctor, everything is fenced in because they say they're going to put in a PEMEX station."

"And then what happened?"

"The natural thing to happen, of course, doctor. I'm surprised that you didn't guess. I started to get excited. Cato climbed up on a really young *burra* close to the *huizache* where I was hidden. Look, right over there is where the *huizache* I'm talking about must have been. I talk and talk, and you write and write, without making a sound, on those pumpkin-colored sheets you have. All of this feels like it was yesterday, doctor."

"Go on, please go on."

"The point is that this guy Catalino, or Cato as everybody knew him, got up onto a rock to reach the little *burra*. He took out his two corncobs from his pocket and tossed them on the ground in front of the animal."

"This seems completely made up. Like from a movie."

"I don't know if it could be from a movie or made up like you say, doctor, but everything I'm telling you is exactly what I saw and what I remember. If you don't want to write down what I'm telling you, that's your problem. Here in Purísima it's reality. Maybe up there in the United States, it might sound made up or like a movie. The same thing happens when I tell stories about the United States here in Purísima. They don't believe everything you suffer when you're a wetback in the United States."

"Like I told you before, I got excited and that made me really happy because I realized that when those junior high kids salted my Johnson it was all just bullshit. Cato thrust harder and harder against the creature. The *burrica* didn't do anything but twitch her ears once in a while to shoo away a fly or two. The little *burra's* eyes looked like two black, black mirrors. In the glass of her eyes it looked like you could lose all of the damned worries in the world."

"Now I'm getting to the point, Dr. Smith, which is that that was the first day that I had relations. I did it with the *burrica* because I wanted to prove to myself that the salting was just a big lie that the kids made up. Yes, doctor, that was the first and only time that I had relations with anyone.

Well, you probably know better than me, but whether I feel guilty, I sure do feel bad about doing it with such a gentle little animal like that little *burra*. I'm not going to get into the whole thing about God, doctor. If the Bible says that it's a sin, then let God condemn me for my weakness. That's fine, doctor. I promise that this very Sunday I'll go to confession at the church for this enormous sin I committed."

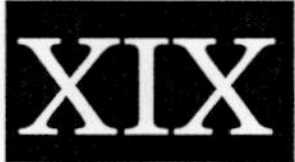

The Ranch House Garden

Heads up! The Jehovah's Witnesses are here!" yelled Goodnight, who kept on shaving his head beneath the shade of the fig tree. In the shattered mirror, Goodnight, still running the knife over his scalp, made out through the foam pieces of ties, flowered dresses, bicycle handles and helmets.

Goodnight turned to his left and continued to scrape with the blade that was uncovering the snake-like scar that he had on his skull. Two years ago he had hit his head on a ladder while he was picking Kings of Diamonds. Since then, he talks to himself all the time. He chats with the trees, he invites the August Ladies to dance, he says goodbye to them, and he tells them goodnight at high noon. The other workers say that he had a "me attack." Goodnight cleaned off the knife on his left arm, laughed in front of the mirror, and his earth-colored face went to pieces.

"We are Jehovah's Witnesses. We bring good news from Jehovah."

"Goodnight! I am Goodnight. Did you just say that these are the new Jehovah's white girls? By God, the damned gals are just gorgeous! Guys, guys, the hallelujah brothers are here to talk to you! Goodnight! Goodnight! Go on through, whities! Go right ahead. Welcome to Eden."

The Ranch House garden was full of earthen statues. Selma had been showing her creative side with water and mud. The days she didn't work, she would spend hours and hours spreading the mud in the garden. On the huge mud canvases, using a little stick she would draw faces with sad expressions, with enormous eyes and mouths. She drew suns, moons, corn, jaguars, eagles, feathers, magueys, cactus, flowers, and strange symbols that nobody understood. Little Clown loved to watch Selma work the chalky earth. He would sit on a tree trunk for hours and hours just gazing at the figures Selma made. Sobbing, he would smoke cigarettes and then start writing on a sheaf of paper. Nobody knew why he would cry when he looked at the clay figures.

By now every inch of the garden was covered by drawings. On top of the first figures, Selma started to build crosses, swords, horses, churches, boats, and all kinds of saints. Silvino and Rosalío especially liked those figures. In the afternoon they would kneel on the ground and say prayers to the religious forms.

Our Father who art in Heaven. Hallowed be thy name. Thy kingdom come, thy will be done, on Earth as it is in Heaven. In the name of the Father, the Son, and the Holy Ghost, Amen.

One morning the Ranch House garden greeted the sun tattooed with modern buildings. The crosses on the churches had been almost erased by the huge M's of the McDonald's restaurants. The image of the Virgin of Guadalupe was halfway obscured by the big letters spelling out HOLLYWOOD. The magueys ended up decorated with an aura made out of large letters that said Coca-Cola. Over the marigolds there was a maternity ward.

That morning, the workers came out into the garden and stared in confusion. They were thrown off balance by the spectacle of all the new etchings. The garden floor had been transformed into a collage of time and space. The workers looked like the turkeys that people take to the city and for lack of space store on the patio, and one day without warning they waddle up to the highest place on the patio and stare in confusion at the spectacle of a monstrous city.

Three months later, Selma started to draw the American continent. She took pains to draw exactly the divisions between each of the states of Mexico. The workers argued because some of them said that Texas, New Mexico, California, Arizona, Colorado, and Utah weren't part of Mexico. Others said that they were, but that the United States had stolen them, and others said that the Mexican government had sold them for fifteen million dollars. Selma came over to the other workers and told them that the lands of this continent belonged to nobody but the indigenous people. They didn't understand and kept on arguing anyway. Selma drew a very precise line that completed the map of Mexico. In big letters she wrote the word BORDER.

Over these letters she started making figures of naked women. These weren't merely drawings etched into the clay of the border, they were sculptures. She spent hours and hours making enormous vats of mud, and in a few days she had filled the middle of the garden with clay dolls. They were figures of women with big breasts and narrow hips. Clay dolls posed in different positions: prenatal, on all fours, looking at the stars, on their backs, on their bellies.

Selma had just done giving her sculptures the finishing touches the day that the Jehovah's Witnesses arrived at the Ranch House. The breasts and buttocks of the clay dolls shined brightly with the last touch of water and Selma's subtle strokes with the pads of her fingers.

After her dabbling Selma went walking among the orchards. The workers, faster than a cock could crow, got buck-naked and each one of them let himself be drawn to the mud dolls like moths to a flame. One of them made a hole in the one that was in doggy position and thrust his manhood into the clay. On the other side of the garden, another was sucking at the pointed clay teats of another sculpture. Further away, Scarface was clutching at the doll that was lying face up. Cholver and Cuerna were throwing things around in the muddy mire of the garden. Their seventy year-old earth-colored flesh looked even older next to the erotic shine of the clay women. Cholver and Cuerna looked like two boys having the best time. Nobody had ever seen them so happy as they were on that day. They amused themselves slapping their buddies on the ass, who no more than frowned at the feel of the wrinkled hands. Cholver and Cuerna, out of their heads crazy, rolled around in the clay. They kicked. They were ecstatic. They burst out laughing to see their buddies coming to orgasm inside the damp clay of the figures.

The Jehovah's Witnesses walked into the Ranch House garden. They were all clean and dressed up for the job of converting the black sheep of the Ranch House to the Protestant faith. The two young ladies and the young man stood like turkeys gawking at that scenario of mud and men. Bodies and clay mingled together as if they both were one and the same stuff. Chicho still was embracing the earth. The doll already had disintegrated into a mass of clay, but his mind continued on the same track, to come to climax. He got up dribbling sperm, and you only could see his teeth in his face covered with clay. That was the last image that the Jehovah's Witnesses saw at the Ranch House.

"Goodnight, folks. I'm Goodnight. Here you have the Jehovah's whities. Go right on through, whities, to the Ranch House Eden."

The Jehovah's Witnesses never dared to give their testimony as to what they had seen that afternoon in the Ranch House garden.

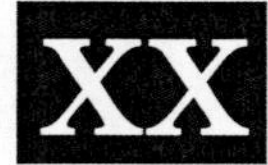

Terrestre Mora

"Border Patrol! Border Patrol! Run, run, run!"

The workers climbed down their ladders ready to take off running. The foreman Clemente Furia Jr., as soon as he saw them run, let out a guffaw that sufficed to tell the workers that it had been just a joke.

"I thought you weren't going to run, Panchito! You were the first one down from your ladder."

"Don't flap your mouth, Furia. I barely came down one step. Like I told you, I'm going to do what Terrestre Mora did."

"You better hope that the same thing doesn't happen to you that happened to your great-grandfather. If you want to pull a Terrestre Mora, you'd better start practicing leaping like a tiger and saying 'I am U.S. Citizen Sir,' because so far you hop like a monkey and not even you understand your own runaway English."

"Now you're gonna start with that. Hey, I already know how to say 'My name is Frank and…'"

"Panchito!" one of his coworkers yelled. "Don't be a son of a Budweiser and get back to work, because I'm not picking up the slack for any lazy bastard."

"Shut your fucking mouth, fat-ass *burra*! Don't stick your nose in other people's business."

"What?" all of the other workers cried in unison.

"Eat this, you bastards!" retorted Panchito, waving a long, thick branch that he just had pruned off of the King of Diamonds peach tree.

"Save that for digging your grave," responded Burra.

They broke out into a furious game of verbal one-upsmanship until one of them came out clearly as the winner, Burra. The field hands could get pretty upset when the verbal sparring started into the sexual harassment of family members.

"I did your sister."

"I'm ringing your bell."

"Leave the bell for the church and your sister, why don't you."

The moment would come when words lost their meaning. Even a "Here comes the Border Patrol, run!" from Clemente Furia Jr. didn't scare anybody at that hour of exhaustion. No matter how violent the word-slinging got then, nobody took offense, and the sayings would get lost among the creaking of the branches being pruned. By this time Panchito didn't even respond when Burra used the worst language possible to talk about his entire family. At that time of the afternoon, you only could hear Panchito's low murmur. It was like a mental prayer, his repetition of the phrase "I'm U.S. Citizen Sir" that dribbled out stickily with the white saliva on his lips.

* * *

The Border Patrol didn't show up just like that by coincidence. Without a doubt somebody had blown the whistle, thought Terrestre Mora when he heard one of his fellow workers blast out with "Border Patrol, *La Migra*, run everybody, run!" Thirty field hands, women, men, and children scattered among the trees of the King of Diamonds orchard. The Border Patrol agents started their human hunt. Clemente Furia Sr., still the foreman then, sat in his truck and observed the whole scene from behind dark glasses. He rolled down the window, took off his shades, and showed his Resident Alien card to the agent, who then checked to make sure there weren't any undocumented immigrants hiding under the seats. The agent walked away from the truck, and Furia slid his glasses back on, as if he were afraid that his eyes were going to reveal some sort of complicity with the look that Terrestre Mora sent him from up on his ladder. In that instant, Furia remembered the oath that Mora had taken one day in the Ranch House.

"I swear on my mother and on this…" Mora made the sign of the cross with his thumb and index finger, then kissed the tips of his fingers, "that never in my life will I run from *La Migra*."

Clemente Furia Sr. wore himself out making fun of him. He laughed so long and hard that he had to hold onto his belly so his sides wouldn't split. Now Furia felt that laughter turning into a ball of rage in his stomach and wished with all of his heart that the Border Patrol agents would kick the shit out of Mora and drag him into the dog cage. Even Mora's presence got on the foreman's nerves. He felt like the guy's dark eyes followed him everywhere and he had a feeling that Mora knew about some of the tricks that he was pulling on the workers.

Mora, without losing his calm, worked his shears harder and harder, while he muttered through gritted teeth, "Fucking huge trees that end up being mine. They're as big as a mesquite… yeah, the size of a mesquite tree, and then they don't pay us more than twenty-five cents for each one."

Only six workers, including Mora, continued clipping the King of Diamond branches at the top of their 18-foot ladders. Three of the Border Patrol agents started to check their papers. Pedro Coras, his two buddies Gabriel Armenta and Lucio García, Doña Carmelita García Díaz and Carolino Pérez silently waited on their ladders for the agents to check their papers, because they all had their Resident Alien cards.

"Get out of here, Morita! These dogs are gonna eat you alive. Take off!" Carolino Pérez whispered to him. "They're on their way over now, go on, get the hell out of here!"

"I'm not afraid of those dogs. Who do they think they are, for me to be afraid of them? I suppose they don't have to wipe when they take a shit?" thought Mora seconds before they came up to check his papers.

You could hear the *pshhh* of somebody opening a coke. Furia lifted the can to his mouth, expecting to taste the sweetness of the refreshing liquid, but only felt a bitter and foamy aftertaste at the back of his throat.

A chubby agent walked over to Terrestre Mora. In that instant Furia rolled his window the rest of the way down and sputtered, "Now we'll see if you really won't run, you big son of a bitch."

The Border Patrol biplane droned above the Kings of Diamonds. Mora felt as if the blades of his pruning shears had grown and he felt like his arms were as strong as two steel rods. The plane passed over his head, and he felt like the sound shot through his eardrums like metal thread. Now he was pruning practically on autopilot. You could see the sweat coursing down his neck, the fluid drenching his armpits. All of a sudden he started to feel a chill passing through his entire body. Just then he wished he could take his shears and with one slash make mincemeat out of that plane.

"Son of a whoredog, now you've ruined that Diamond!" Clemente Furia Sr. said between clenched teeth.

Impatiently the three agents shook the ladder, so that Terrestre Mora's pruning shears dropped to one side and then he plummeted as if he had fainted from shock. The agents waited for him to take off running like a cornered rabbit. But nothing. Not a thing. Terrestre didn't even attempt to move an inch when they started kicking him harder and harder in the ribs. His body remained motionless, tensed and stuck to the ground like a little piece of metal on an enormous magnet. It was as if the earth was calling him. Like he belonged to the earth, or the earth belonged to him. For just a moment the agents thought he was dead. He had fallen so hard that they didn't doubt that he could have died instantaneously. And thus things stood until the second round of kicking. He gave a sign of life, and that's when his friends realized that he was still alive.

Without complaining, he started to shift and then to hug the earth with such strength that it looked like the earth was making him dig to get six feet under. Scraping fiercely, desperately, he plunged his hands into the dirt until he reached a thick and ancient root. The chunky agent started to jerk at him, but Mora seemed to be pulled by unknown forces. The fat guy, who by now was pissed off, heaved at him by the shoulders, but ended up falling on his ass onto some branches. He got up and started to pull again to drag him out of the earth, but only managed to yank his shirt off. Terrestre, biting at the sandy earth, sank his head deeper into the ground as if he were a mole. The other two Border Patrol agents got goose bumps hearing the sandy crunching between Mora's teeth.

The fat man, panting and sweating like a pig, grabbed Mora's shoulders and tugged even harder, with no result. He managed to stick his fat, pink, soft hands under Mora's greasy armpits and thought, "Now I've got you, you damned groundhog." The other agents started to be amused by the whole scene and between joking and serious begged their colleague to pull harder.

Terrestre Mora's nostrils were plugged up with mud, and he started having difficulty breathing. He raised his face in order to spit and take in a breath or two, but without letting go of the old root.

"Goddamned groundhog! I have you now!" he yelled, his plump chin shaking.

The agent grabbed him by the hair and pulled hard, but it was futile. He fell on his ass yet again with a lock of hair in his fist. Almost out of breath by now, he got up, sucked in some air, and one more time set himself to getting Mora off of the ground.

Terrestre Mora felt a great deal of moisture around his hands. The earth was well-watered and muddy. He felt lost. He felt like the earth was betraying him. The fat man yanked hard on one arm, and the King of Diamonds gave its first shiver. One pull… two pulls… three pulls… and Mora still held on to the earth. Between the three agents, they gave a mighty tug. The King of Diamonds creaked, and so did Mora. Both sounds rang as one in the ears of everybody there.

Thirty field hands already were inside of the dog cages, and the airplane already had flown away. The rest of the agents were coming back where the three were having difficulties with one of the wetbacks. The fat guy explained what had happened to his boss, who straightened his cowboy hat, put on his shades, and took a last puff on his cigarette. Pissed off, he threw down the butt and stamped it out, then spit on Mora's back.

"What country are you from?" the boss asked Mora in perfect Spanish. "Are you from El Salvador, Guatemala… where are you from?"

Mora held up his right hand to signal that he wanted to say something, fearful that they would pull him arms off if they pulled one more time. "He's from Mexico. He's a Mexican like the rest of us; you can see the M on the palm of his hand. The M for Mexico." Carolino considered saying this to the agent in charge, for fear that they would deport Mora to some other country, but the words stuck in his throat. Carolino Pérez swallowed spit when he saw Mora's hand dripping with blood.

The palm of Mora's hand had been skinned completely, from his wrist to the tips of his fingers. The blood ran bubbling down to his armpit. His fingers had lost their fingernails, their pads, their flesh... Only the cartilage remained, clenched.

"Where are you from, boy? Do you speak English?" asked the boss, showing his own bilingual capacity.

"*I'm U.S. Citizen, Sir.*" Between his teeth he began to chew the phrase that he had learned by heart and repeated constantly every day as he worked. Now was the moment to spit out this phrase in English as cleanly as possible. He wanted to get it out of himself, but it stuck between the muddy roof of his mouth and his tongue like some enormous yellow gob of phlegm. The "*I'm U.S. Citizen, Sir*" was there clear as day in his mind but not on his lips. This was exactly the time to toss out that phrase, as muddy, bloody, or spiteful it might be, and to jab it right in the ears of the Border Patrol and Clemente Furia Sr.

"Bastard, like hell, *I'm U.S. Citizen, Sir.*" Said Furia as he crushed the aluminum can with one hand and threw it into the recycling bin.

The agent in charge ordered shovels brought to dig Mora out of the ground. But before they started the excavation, Mora started making an effort to stutter a few words. The agents listened hard, as if to say "What's that he's saying?"

"I think he's speaking English, " said the chubby one.

"I'm a U.S. Citizen, Sir." Terrestre Mora pronounced in perfect English. The Border Patrol boss felt his balls shrink out of fear of a lawsuit for violating the human rights of an American citizen.

Mora lifted up his head, shook it, and spit out a strong steam of black liquid, followed by a flood of phrases in English that he had memorized from some of the pamphlets that the Jehovah's Witnesses had left one day. Mora recited by heart Isaiah 35:5 and 6, Isaiah 14:7 and Psalm 37:11. Nobody noticed that each of the Biblical quotes had been altered, each having been changed to the negative. Finally he recited Isaiah 65:17, taking away the negative. Terrestre Mora's correctly pronounced English left the agents, his five buddies who had kept on pruning, and Clemente Furia Sr. with their jaws hanging open.

The agents absconded from the King of Diamonds orchard leaving Mora in the same position, holding on to the ground. The boss made a brief speech to the rest of the agents before they left. They would have to cover up any sort of evidence of wrongdoing or injustice committed against a United States citizen. The agent in charge was afraid that some fairy reporter from the county might find out what happened. It was absolutely mandatory to say that they had never been in the area. That they had found the thirty undocumented aliens close to the river in an abandoned shack, all scratching their balls, something that according to popular knowledge all wetbacks knew how to do.

* * *

The "*I'm a U.S. Citizen, Sir,*" by late afternoon, Panchito was repeating it over and over just in his head, because if he tried to open his mouth, his lips would bleed they were so dry. He went over and over the magic phrase that his grandfather Vidalino García had told him, who had heard the story from his old friend Carolino Pérez, about how it saved the life of a God-fearing illegal immigrant. Panchito closed his shears violently around a thick branch of the King of Diamonds that he was pruning and felt a horrible pain in his right arm. It's a damn *huevonada*, thought Panchito as he saw the mound of nerves swell in his right arm. His lips had torn apart involuntarily and the first thing he did was spit out the blood, then he came down from the ladder holding tightly onto his arm with his other hand. He squatted down and howled so everyone could hear, it's a *huevonada*! Everybody started shouting at the same time, "a *huevonada*, a *huevonada*! Who's got it?"

"Who wants to get rid of his *huevonada*? " asked the foreman Clemente Furia Jr. "Not you, Burra, because you already busted open three this season."

"Now you're going to start with that again. When I was going to get Pepe's *huevonada*, remember that it was you who picked out the switch. The fucking switch was no good," protested Burra.

Panchito wanted Virginio to give him the treatment with a whippy switch that his friend Manuel cut off of a King of Diamonds. Virginio lashed the switch three times in the wind before using it to treat the seized-up nerves in Panchito's arm. But they had to wait ten minutes because the *gringo*, the owner of the orchards, felt like observing how his workers cured their Mexican *huevonadas*. The workers waited quietly in a circle for the boss to show up, while Panchito writhed in agony.

"Oh, mucho dolor, amigo!" the gringo's round pink face uttered when he saw Virginio slash open Panchito's arm.

Within half an hour Panchito was back to pruning. Virginio had broken up the nerve spasm switching it repeatedly with the branch. Panchito felt a pain that went from the base of his neck all the way down his spine.

* * *

It was three minutes before four o'clock in the afternoon when the Border Patrol snuck up on Clemente Furia Jr.'s troop as they were pruning. A few had time to take off running. The others didn't have time to make a peep, and resignedly climbed down the last six steps of their ladders, hands behind their heads.

One agent approached the tree where Panchito was working, and he threw himself down onto the ground from the last step of the ladder and when he fell he screamed, because his *huevonada* came back. In spite of the pain he started digging with his fingernails and teeth, in search of a root that would save him from being deported. Two strong, muscled agents jumped on him and got him up with a series of kicks. Panchito's mind went blank and as hard as he tried he couldn't remember the magic phrase that once had saved a God-fearing illegal worker from deportation. After they had him in handcuffs he managed to sputter something like, "U.S. Ser… No Espanish."

"SHUT UP, GREASER!"

They tossed him in the dog cage like a stray mutt with rabies. Panchito's sobs stopped cold at the slam of the green and white door.

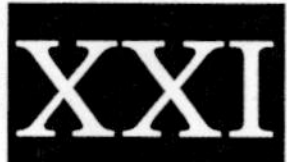

Elegant Ladies

One day in the month of July, somewhere around noon, the contractor Ramiro Ramírez arrived at the Elegant Ladies orchard to bring us a huge cooler of ice-cold water. The contractor loved to see so many boxes already packed with Elegant Ladies peaches. Between the twenty workers, we already had filled up eighty crates of picked peaches.

"Very *bueno*, Clemente! Very *buen trabajo*, amigos! See you *mañana*!"

The night before, at the Ranch House, Mateo had told us that the company was giving Clemente Furia Jr. twenty five dollars for each crate of fruit, when he only was giving us ten bucks a box. We workers just sat there quiet, not knowing what to say. We tried to calm our rage by picking faster. In a snap of the fingers we were up and down the ladder with our pack filled up with Elegant Ladies peaches. The first worker to fill up his pack would yell out a challenge for all of us to go and empty out our bags into the crates. We worked in a state of euphoria.

"Fuck your momma whatever bastard doesn't come to empty out his bag, and fuck your momma if you don't have your pack full!"

"Well, fuck your momma whoever is the last man back up his ladder!"

"And fuck your momma if you can't come empty your pack again now!"

"And any bastard who's picking little green fruit, you're a son of a whoredog!" shouted Clemente Furia Jr., swearing at us.

That noon in the month of July was sweltering between the heat and humidity of the earth, which had just been irrigated. Chapo looked like he was getting a heat stroke. He kneeled down to drink water, but no sooner had he taken a sip when he fell to his hands and knees on the ground. He had passed out. Chicho and Kalimán rolled him over under one of the trees and with their caps they fanned him so he would come to. He came to, but his nose started bleeding.

"See, you fucking drug addicts! That's what's going to happen to all of you if you keep snorting that cocaine up your noses," yelled old Clemente Furia Sr.

"Shut your mouth, you stupid old man! What do you know, you're not the foreman any more, you're just one more worker under my command," answered Clemente Furia Jr.

"I know more than you do! You think I don't know that a bunch of these idiots are drug addicts just like you."

"If you hadn't yanked me out of school, I wouldn't be here right now working myself to death under this sun," he reproached his father resentfully.

"Son of a bitch, here they go one more time with the same old story," Old Andrade commented under his breath.

"The two of them are at it again, fucking shithole family," muttered Ramplas to himself.

"I took you out of school because we had to work if we wanted to fill our bellies. You know that your mother was a whore. One day she took off to play around in the bars and left you behind with me. I had to change your diapers and make sure you had something to eat."

"Yeah, yeah, my momma was a whore and probably still is, but why did that mean you had to take me out of school? By this time I'd be all dressed up, working in an office with air conditioning and earning a shitload of money. No, but some guy dumber than dirt got the bright idea of taking his son out of school to go pick garlic. Fucking worthless garlic!"

"You can be such an asshole! I pulled you out of school because we didn't even have enough to eat and I wanted to teach you how to work. After we had pulled together a few bucks, I asked you if you wanted to go back to school, and you didn't want to, just remember that."

"You would have sent me back to school for no reason at all! Why were you even asking me if I wanted to go back to school? I didn't even have a green card! I had to buy one on the black market. Look at this fucking card, not worth my dick."

"You're a U.S. citizen. Don't be an asshole."

"And how can I prove it? Let's see, show me a birth certificate that says I was born here. Why didn't you ever get me a social security number? I'm the son of your old whore who you screwed at the border, and so I'm a bastard of my own whore mother who had me on the fucking border. She should have just left me there for the dogs to eat. Everything was going fine until you had the bright idea of taking me to the fucking garlic fields. Oh Almita, Almita, Almita… We'd better change the topic. So why don't you tell me, then, how it was that you met that whore woman of yours, I mean my whore momma."

"Clemente, are you going to get started with that shit again?

"Really, man, give it a rest."

"Yeah, give us all a rest, we've got enough to worry about with these fucking Elegant Ladies."

"Yeah," responded Clemente Furia Jr., "Your whore of a mother is the Elegant Lady, so shut your damn mouth and keep picking."

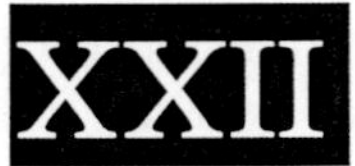

XXII

The Treaty

"*Comadre*, *compadre*, please open the door for us."

"What's the matter, my dear Julia? Why are you pounding on the door at this time of night?" asked the man, who had gotten up in his underwear, as he pulled the bolt of the lock. "Oh my God! What is that body on your mule? Who is dead?"

"It's your godson, Pepe, the devil has come and killed him," answered Julia, enraged. "Yesterday afternoon they came and took Fernando away. Pepe tried to stop them. He no more had jumped on the Rangers who were arresting Fernando, and started hitting them, when one of them shot him three times in the back."

"Oh my God, that breaks my heart! I'm always telling my husband that we should leave before they kill us," cried the woman who had just gotten up.

"I'm going to Saltillo to live with one of my sisters."

"Don't go, *comadre*. They signed that treaty to end the war. Things are going to change. I heard tell that there treaty is gonna protect us too. They say that we got the same rights as all the citizens round these parts."

"The end of the war, you say, *compadre*? That treaty is just the beginning… The beginning of a never-ending war between Mexicans and

Gringos. One day to the next they changed all the land markers on us. Now the border has crossed us. It's left us all branded for the rest of our lives."

"You've gotta have faith in the treaty, *comadre*."

"Faith? How can I have faith if they have left me empty inside in just one day? They take my husband prisoner, they kill my thirteen year-old son, and they demolish my house. You should have seen how much hate they put in to destroying my little altar to the Virgin of Guadalupe and the Saints."

"Excuse me for sticking my nose in, *comadre*, but if you will let us, we can have Pepe's wake in our house, and tomorrow we will help you give him a decent burial in holy ground," begged her *compadre*, weeping.

"No, not here! Those shameless good-for-nothings are capable of coming and digging up the entire area to take him out and throw his remains in the garbage. Right this minute I'm taking him to Saltillo. I want to bury him there."

"But this is his home. He was born here and he lived his thirteen years here, and you should bury him here, *comadre*."

"I've been thinking about it all night. Fernando and I were so sure that we should die fighting for what belongs to us, but you see what happened. If I bury Pepe in occupied Mexico, Fernando is never going to want to leave, and then they'll end up killing me or our other son, the one that I'm carrying in my womb. If you see Fernando, tell him that I went to my sister's in Saltillo. He'll do what he has to do."

The couple lowered their eyes in respect of their godson's body. Between sobs and tears they hugged their *comadre* Julia goodbye. The two sat down on a mesquite log. From there they watched their friend disappear in a cloud of dust as she trudged south. They stayed there until the violent howl of a dog shook them out of their reverie.

* * *

On December 12, 1848, the Rangers arrived at the Mora family ranch. Mr. Mora had just finished putting an edge on the blade of his axe. Without moving a muscle, Octavio Mora watched the nine Rangers come in with their cudgels. The dog started to howl and the chickens started a big ruckus in the corral.

At the entryway of the house, Señora Agustina Mora finished emptying a jar of peppers into the pot of hominy stew, which she was making for dinner. When she saw the Rangers she dropped the lid to the pot and ran to pick up her three year-old son that was playing close to the blood-red perennials, drawing lines in the earth with a mesquite branch.

Octavio, as if he was ignoring the presence of the Rangers, started to make firewood out of the mesquite log. The doves, pigeons and swallows, perched on the piles of manure in the corral, were going after the splinters that flew at the contact of metal and wood. Fighting each other they pecked at the slivers of wood and then, disappointed they weren't worms or grain, they left them on the manure. As a flock they came and went following the splinters along the border line, painted down the middle of the Mora property.

Three heavy blows knocked Octavio Mora to the ground. He tried to get up quickly, but a flurry of kicks landed all over his body. "You disgusting pig… we warned you three times… these lands belong to us on account of Manifest Destiny… don't you dare cross that line…" were the words that rained from the Rangers' mouths as they continued to beat the shit out of the man coiled up at their feet.

Between three of the Rangers they tried to pick him up and throw him over the painted white line. They couldn't manage to get him off the ground because Mora was hugging the mesquite log for all he was worth. Enraged, the Rangers let fly another bout of kicks at Mora's ravaged body.

Agustina, infuriated, fatally wounded one of the lawmen with a blast from her shotgun. She tried to get off another shot, but a blow from the butt of a rifle knocked her to the floor. She received another blow to her head. Three Rangers tossed her over the line as if she were a bag of bones. Another Ranger grabbed the boy and threw him angrily over the line to where his mother lay.

Octavio Mora was still holding onto the mesquite trunk. It took six Rangers to pick him up along with the mesquite log and heave them both over the line. Mora still had his arms around the log. Because the terrain was so uneven, body and log started to roll toward the white boundary. Octavio, perhaps without even knowing it, crossed the frontier for the first and last time. Or maybe that border crossed him, for good.

The Rangers, out of their minds with rage, decided to finish the game for once and for all. One of them took Octavio Mora's hatchet. The first slash cut four fingers of his hand. A second one cut all five off the other hand. Nine jumping fingers whirled in a pond of blood straddling a purple line.

With pomp and majesty an eagle landed on a metal post that marked a new border. Immediately the flock of birds, that had been inching closer to peck at the blood clots, went into a frenzy. Scared to death of the Imperial Eagle, the birds dispersed over to the corral that happened to be in occupied Mexico, among the Mexican brush.

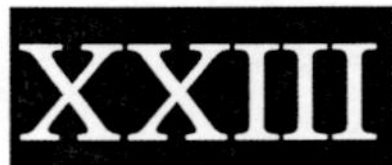

White-out

When the thinning season is over, about halfway through the month of April, the defoliation and whitewashing start right away. These tasks are done practically at the same time. One day we clip off the tender shoots sprouting from the center of the tree, to air out the branches and so that nutrients aren't taken from the unripe fruit. The next day we paint the bark of the nectarine, peach and cherry trees to protect them from the sun. These jobs take about three or four weeks, before the first picking season in May.

* * *

"Radio Campesina! The station by the people and for the people!" The signal came in on Old Andrade's transistor radio and pulled the rest of us out of a deep silence. It was an agonizing silence of brush strokes at the obsidian hour of sacrificial dusk. Andrade took the contraption by the cord and hung it off of his shoulder. I felt my eyes watering as I listened to the music and I went on doing my work with more enthusiasm. The radio made us move our arms up and down with more vigor. By that time of the afternoon I hardly could feel my arms. But how could I get out of it? "En un cofre de vulgar hipocresía..."[5] "Yahoo! We're going strong with this song, a memory of one of the immortal greats of our beautiful and beloved Mexico. But first

---

5 A popular song by Javier Solís, the lyrics say: "In the coffers of vulgar hypocrisy... clown, making the mask of a happy face..."

we want to send out greetings to all of the working men who right now are resting at home. Compatriots, rest well, because tomorrow is going to be a lovely day for work!" "...payaso, con careta de alegría..."

We had been working for fourteen hours whitewashing the August Ladies. In the darkness and inside our tears faded away into the silence. My tears. Our tears and laughs from these tired, invisible bodies. We were spattered from head to toes with the milky liquid that was used to protect the bark of the trees.

At six o'clock in the afternoon the contractor Ramiro Ramirez showed up with the last barrels of whitewash. He climbed out of his brand-new 250F truck as happy as can be. Always wearing his dark glasses and chewing that toothpick, as if he had just finished eating a good plate of roast. Ramiro called the milky liquid "white-out."

Erasing. Painting...painting... I wished that in one instant I could paint with one stroke the entire orchard of August Ladies just so I could rest my back over the raised earth around one of the trees. But we had to go on erasing and erasing. Erasing. Painting... painting... Painting up to the sky in the color of milk if I could, just so I could throw the damn bucket to hell. Paint our Mexican faces? Paint our features? Features like earth, cracked like the clay in a dry creek bed. "White-out" our faces, that in the mornings framed the gleaming white of our teeth? Erasing, erasing, erasing the past that belonged to us? We had to erase the sun's tracks with "white-out" as if the trees were lines on one of the documents forged by the contractor Ramirez.

It was so easy for Ramirez to use the White-out in his office, inventing numbers and giving us artistically creative names. Ramirez invented Social Security numbers for us, which later he would claim as his own. He too received some of our unemployment benefits and tax returns.

"Your name is going to be José Alfredo Jiménez. You Mario Moreno. You Camilo Sexto."[6]

But those of us who were working, how could we erase our exhaustion? How could we erase the crevices of our indigenous past, out of which arose our resistance to these long days?

---

6 Jiménez and Sexto are nationally beloved singers, and Moreno is the actor who plays Cantinflas in the wildly popular series of movies.

"They look just like Indians!" Ramirez would say to the foreman Clemente Furia. Why didn't he say "We"? They, those guys, always that one or the other. Ramirez with his face like a pestle and his Cortez style goatee, he would say that like he was looking at some impressionist painting, "The Harvest" by Lhermitte. What part of him drew him to delight in and join the painting? What part kept him distant? Was it that damn runaway English that he chattered with foreman Furia that made him feel like he was milk from the same barrel? Was it his new Ford the company provided him, or his power in the central office? Was it his get-up of dark glasses, leather boots, jeans and cowboy shirts, silk bandana around his neck, toothpick, walkie-talkie, and knife stuck in its sheath that made him feel like he wasn't part of our painting?

"Clemente, you think it will be enough to finish tonight Damas de Agosto?" asked Ramirez.

"Ummm, I think..." stammered Furia as he glanced over at the barrels and then turned toward the August Ladies as if he was making a mathematical calculation, although to tell the truth he didn't know how to multiply or read for that matter. "Yes, va a ser enough."

"Bueno, muy bueno. See you mañana in Damas Elegantes!"

Our spirit during those long days of labor was like Old Andrade's radio. In the morning and at night we came in just perfectly. There wasn't a single worker who wouldn't give out a yell when he heard a song by Lucha Villa, José Alfredo, Pedro Infante. Was it a yell of joy, of pain, of melancholy? Only God knows what those yells really meant.

Every once in a while some of the guys would tell a joke, or others would cuss each other out. At all of this, Furia would occasionally let fall an ironic smile from his evil-looking face.

* * *

"Chicho, tell one of your stories!" the foreman Clemente Furia urged the only worker who dared to talk to him like an equal.

"I got your story right here!"

"That's great, but move those hands."

"Look, you can't even see them."

"Well, you must have them hidden in your pocket or some shit."

"No way, man! I'm telling you that you can't see them from how thick I'm painting on the milk."

"Yeah, call me later."

"Hey, man! Don't be like that. I was serious. Look how I can finish a branch before you can blink! A brush in each hand. Out of curiosity, do you happen to have an extra brush over there?"

"Why?"

"So I can paint this stuff with my ass too!" The other field hands cracked up laughing. "I'm just joking! I don't need another brush, because if I'm going to tell a story I have to use my hands. Let me stick the mop here in the tree so I can get ready to tell you a good one."

"Chicho, I think you're full of shit. What you want is a break so I'll offer you a toke on a joint, huh?" Clemente Furia gave us all permission to stop working while Chicho got ready to tell his tale.

We took advantage of the chance to set down the weight of the buckets. Some sat down with their legs crossed and some of us just squatted down on our haunches. We all gathered around in a circle while the guys lit up their Marlboros to get the most out of the yarn that the storyteller Chicho was going to spin. But before he started, he rolled up a marijuana cigarette.

"Go ahead and start, fucking Chicho," ordered Furia, running his tongue over the paper before lighting the joint. This was like a ritual for Clemente Furia, who even licked his Marlboros.

"One day the Mexican people asked the Gringos to share with them all of their knowledge of science and philosophy of the cosmos," Chicho started recounting. "The Gringos laughed and told them no, because their race was still too backward. The Mexicans got super pissed off and challenged them to a duel of philosophical battle. They said that they would put their best philosophers up against each other to see once and for all who was the biggest badass. The Gringos accepted the challenge, so they made a plan to meet on December 24, up in the White House."

"You bastard! I thought you said you needed both hands to tell the fucking story!" reminded Furia as he passed him the joint. "You aren't using them for anything but to burn your fingernails on this!"

"But wait! Here comes the good part," said Chicho, as if he was getting ready to walk onto a set. And it was almost like that, because he set his cap on backward, burned his fingernails once more like he liked to say, and went on with the tale.

"The Mexicans were up a creek. They were like rats in a maze. They didn't know how they were going to fare, because there wasn't a single kick-ass philosopher in all of Mexico. Finally the day of the philosophical duel in the White House arrived, and *La Raza* still hadn't found anybody. At the last minute they thought of passing by a little town in Michoacán, where they ran into José Francisco Chilotes. Chilotes was a bigger bullshitter than the devil himself. On that particular day Chilotes was running a little short, and with the big shindig they offered him, they convinced him in a heartbeat. They went *en masse* flying López Portillo's Quetzalcoatl and they didn't stop until they reached the *Estamos Hundidos*.[7] They dressed Chilotes up in some second-hand finery to cover up his badass look. He took a shot of tequila and made the sign of the cross, and he said, "So now I have kept the promise I made to the Virgin of Guadalupe. I promised her I would go to the United States and think of her in the land of the Gabachos on her very Saint's Day."

"The Gringo philosopher was dressed to the nines and quickly came to the front, but Chilotes looked like the real thing with his three-month beard and his lawyer bifocals that somebody had lent him. His eyes were bloodshot from a bad hangover, but the Gringos thought that he was burning up his lashes reading so much. But the only thing Chilotes knew how to burn were his fingernails."

"The Gringos asked what language the philosophers were going to use for the duel. The Mexicans pretended to huddle with Chilotes. Then they told the Gringos that Chilotes had said that it was all the same to him if they communicated in Greek, Latin, English, or Spanish, but he preferred

---

7 López Portillo, former President of Mexico, preferred to travel in his private airplane, painted all white to match his everpresent all-white suit. He flew so frequently that people joked he was like the Aztec God Quetzalcoatl in being half earth, have air. *Estamos Hundidos* is a word play on *Estados Unidos*, or United States, literally meaning "We are sunk."

sign language, being the language of true philosophers. The Gringos were stunned and went to consult with their number one guy, who was a little taken aback, but accepted the terms. Then the battle of signs began between Chilotes and the suit."

"And then what?" asked Furia. "This is already the second doobie. Don't take too long, because the big boss could show up any fucking minute."

"The Gringo stood up," continued Chicho. "Everybody was hanging on every move he made, and all you could hear was the thunder of cameras for all the photos that were being taken from all sides. The Gringo held up his index finger and the whole crowd had their jaws hanging open, except for Chilotes, who in that very moment was shifting his jacket so you couldn't see the bottle of rotgut whiskey he had tucked away."

"Chilotes took a step forward and then made as of to hike up his trousers. He stared at the Gringo, who still had his index finger in the air, and Chilotes raised his index finger, his middle finger, and his thumb. The Gringo responded sticking up his index finger, but this time waving it around in circles. Chilotes gazed at him and stuck up his own index finger again, but he held it out making the motion of a piston, going up and down."

"The Gringo showed him his arm, with the palm of his hand open. Chilotes immediately held up his hand clenched into a fist. The Gringo philosopher hung his head and told the rest of the Gringos that the Mexicans deserved the prize because they had risen to a very high understanding of the laws of the universe. They went off and talked by themselves so they could ask him about the meaning of those signs.

"The Gringo said to them, 'I told him with my index finger that there is only one God. The Mexican responded that this was true, and holding up his index finger, middle finger, and thumb he said that this was the Holy Trinity. Spinning my finger around I said that God is everywhere, and he replied that this was true, but that God comes and goes between Heaven and earth as well. I said with the palm of my hand that God is love, and he responded that God also is power.'"

"So the Gringos gave the Mexicans all of their knowledge of the sciences and philosophy of the cosmos."

"In Los Pinos, the Mexicans threw the mother of all parties. They asked Chilotes about the meaning of those signs. He told them, 'I was trying to get my bottle good and stashed when I saw that damn Gringo telling me with his index finger to stick it. So I told him he would have to use three fingers, he was such a big asshole. Then he said he was going to go round and round with me in the ring, and I said that I was going to stick it to him but good. Finally he replied, saying that he was going to stick it to me with his entire hand. Then I got really pissed off and told him he was a son of a bitch and his mother was a tramp."

The workers cracked up laughing. Only I didn't know if I was laughing or if I was crying because the straps that held the bucket up had rubbed my shoulders bloody. They had been bleeding since the day that we were whitewashing the Sir Georges over by Highway 99.

* * *

We had to stop whitewashing the August Ladies for twenty minutes because the contractor Ramirez hadn't shown up with the barrels of "White-out."

To give my shoulders some respite I squatted at the foot of the trunk that I was whitewashing. And to forget my aches and pains for a while, I started counting the cars that were buzzing by on the freeway. A white Cadillac slowed down and moved over onto the shoulder, but without coming to a stop. Without rolling down the window they took a picture of me, and then two white heads fixed their eyes on me, as I squatted leaning back against the tree, and they shook their heads at me.

The couple in the Cadillac moved back into the lane as they increased their speed. Because of the sizeable racist bumper sticker they had on the back of the car, I figured that it was likely that as they pulled away, they would be attempting to explain the scene that they had just witnessed. They probably would come up with a definition of *them*, *those people* that you find sprawled out all over the country.

Without a doubt the Mister was thinking, *that Mexican...* that we, that I, at the foot of the tree, was the wetback and the violence overtaking the country that he saw every day on television on the Gringo channels. In sum, I would be for him, for them, the lazy Indian wearing rope sandals like the photograph of an indigenous man beside a cactus that I had seen one day in a U.S. magazine. Now he had us, they had us, they had me as one of the lazybones in that bumper sticker proclaiming "South of the Border," stuck on as defense of their car.

For that bejeweled old lady, I was sure that Mexicans symbolized sloth, smuggling, drug addiction, and the burden carried by this country, because undoubtedly she believed that her taxes went to provide for all the Mexicans on welfare.

* * *

"Ok, back to the fucking job. We've had it sweet with the stories, Chicho you sonofabitch," yelled Furia so we would get back to work.

We picked the buckets back up. I was the one who was most affected by the break. My muscles had frozen up on me. I put on the chest harness and hung the bucket by its hooks. The weight of the bucket made me spill the liquid all over my clothes when I would hang it on to the harness. And every time I daubed the whitewash on the higher branches, I got it all over my hair and splashed it in my eyes. I would have to rub my eyes from the stinging. My eyes were already as red as a white rabbit's.

Around three or four in the afternoon, Old Andrade's radio would lose the signal completely. It seemed like the workers resented the radio downtime, because even the most garrulous would stay mute. You would only hear the scuff of the milky brushes against the buckets.

* * *

"...no puedo...soportar mi careta...ante el mundo estoy riendo, y dentro de mi pecho, mi corazón sufriendo, payasoo, payasooo."[8] "Fifteen minutes before eight in the evening, here on your Radio Campesino. The station by the people and for the people. Turn up your radio, so even our Mexican chickens can hear it!"

---

8 The Solís song continues: "I can't...keep up this façade...I laugh for the world and inside my chest my heart suffers, a clownn, a clownnn."

The radio lost the signal again. But we got a hell of a second wind at the last minute.

"We've got two more trees each and then we're done," said Furia, as if that "we" included him. He who didn't touch a bucket or a brush the whole day.

Hearing that, the field hands whitewashed so fast you'd think they never had to paint another tree in their life.

The position of the sun and moon had stopped working like a clock for me since I had come to the Ranch House. As I was whitewashing the last tree, I started to remember how my father's mules would pull harder at the plow when the sun was starting to touch the horizon. Their animal instincts told them that they were getting close to the time to go back to the corral and rest. I recalled how my father would hold up the plow behind the beasts. They would speed up, pushing and pushing harder in that last furrow. Sweating, man and beast pressed victoriously through the open earth.

My father would wipe the sweat from his brow as he watched me in the corral taking off the mules' cinches, reins, bits, harnesses, the chains that held up the plow, and the wooden plow itself.

Walking slowly, my father would approach the clay jug settled among the scarlet flowers in the entryway to drink some water. Meanwhile, the mules would roll around on the manure-strewn corral floor, as if they wanted to scrub both flies and equipment–which wasn't there any more, but which they still could feel on their flesh–off their backs.

My father would ask me to treat the mules' sores. I would take a turkey feather covered in a medicinal paste and swab it on their backs and their hooves. Swarms of flies would land on the poor animals. The flies would drench themselves in blood and medicine, which made them very annoyed, and later they would fall dead on the carpet of dried manure.

My father would sigh happily. My mother, drying her hands on the front of her apron as she came out the front door of the house, would bring a handful of fresh alfalfa for the animals.

Chicho was the first one to finish whitewashing and from sheer joy he flung half a bucket of the liquid into the air. Seconds later we all finished, and having caught his excitement we too hurled our remaining "White-out" in the air. We got out of our harnesses drenched in "White-out" and we threw ourselves down on the ground with our arms stretched out like Christ on the cross.

Clemente took the beer out of the cooler and passed one to each of the workers. They brought them to their lips frantically. I squatted down and with one hand touched the gashes on my shoulders.

Marlboros were lit, and I, who had never smoked a day in my life, accepted one from Old Andrade. I felt like out of our bellies emanated wounded, desperate and furious streams of smoke, like the howl of a badly injured dog. All of our smoke mixed with the milky mist in the wind, soothing the fatigue of our exhausted souls.

I was falling asleep on the ground when I saw the moon appear behind the whitewashed August Ladies. I lifted my eyes to the sky and imagined them as two marbles rolling in my face, like the last two drops of blood of a full moon.

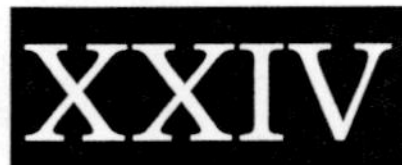

XXIV

The Mute Cow of Harrison Ranch

The Ranch House workers never had been quite so hungry as they were that day. Clemente Furia Jr. had promised to lend them money to buy beans, flour and potatoes, while the thinning season was starting in the nectarine, peach and cherry orchards. Furia hadn't shown up at the Ranch House for a week and a half. Nobody knew that Clemente Furia Jr. was locked up in the clink, they say for driving drunk.

* * *

The night that Clemente Furia was arrested he had a monster hangover like hell from the day before. He went down to the Four of Clubs to freshen up a bit.

"The usual, Clemente?"

"No. Give me a mineral water for now and we'll see about later, and pass me the dice to pass the time over here for a while with Morras."

Furia felt like his head was splitting with all the cigarette smoke and the music cranked up all the way on the jukebox. He drank another bottle of mineral water, but it didn't set well with him at all, so he ran to the bathroom to empty his gut. He stood in front of the mirror, perplexed. He took off his hat and looked closely at his face. His earth-colored face. He got even closer and saw how the mirror fogged up with the vapor of his dragon breath. He rubbed his eyes. He splashed a little water on his face to try to get his senses back, but he didn't feel good and decided that he'd better leave the bar.

He put his truck in gear. Around the corner a patrol car was waiting for him. One of the cops calculated that Clemente Furia must have drunk at least a twelve-pack in the hour and a half that he stayed in the Four of Clubs.

"You see that? He's got his hat on sideways. That's a sign that he's drunk. You show me a Mexican who drives with his cap on sideways and I'll show you a drunk Mexican. It never fails me, just listen to what I'm telling you."

Out of the side street the patrol car slipped out like a ghost from the dark, burning and covered in red and blue flames.

"You are under arrest for driving under the influence of alcohol."

"Give me a blood test so you see I haven't been drinking."

"That's not necessary. I've been watching you for an hour and a half, and you've been drinking at the Four of Clubs. Handcuff that son of a bitch!"

"Damned shameless dogs. I'm taking you to court for being mouthy son of a bitch faggots, *hijos de puta*!"

The police officer, an older man just about to retire, was showing a younger colleague the secrets and tricks of jailing Mexicans. The lesson continued when they left the station house.

"They're weak. They get pissed off immediately if you mention their mother. If you follow them in the black and white, they'll get nervous right away. They start to get out of their lane, drive too slow or too fast, or they just stop the car and get out and run. They do that because they don't have automobile insurance or drivers' licenses, or the car is stolen, or just because they're wetbacks."

"Here comes a car with a headlight out. Are we going to stop him and give him a ticket?"

"No, the driver isn't Mexican. Let's follow him for a minute. You saw already how the driver is dressed. He has on a tie. His headlight probably just went out and he hasn't had time to realize it. He probably just got off of work. Look, he's going toward the north side of the city. The north side is the only part of our city that is worth a damn. Look, he lives there. Let's go back. You see that car that just went by? That driver looks like a Mexican."

"The driver looks awful young, and I think he's exceeding the speed limit a little bit."

"You're learning fast, rookie. Enter the plate into the computer. Look, the car is registered under a woman's name. For sure this guy doesn't even have a license or car insurance, and he's more than likely a wetback. Let's arrest the son of a bitch!"

"I'm just minding my own business. My mother lent me the car to go and pick up my sister from work."

"Shut up, you Greaser! Your momma…"

"Why are you arresting me? Bastards, whoredogs, sons of bitches! Why are you arresting me?"

"I said to shut the hell up, you Greaser!"

"Rookie, the speed limit here is thirty five miles an hour, what would you put as his speed in the report?"

"Forty five."

"I'd put sixty five. After all, neither this snot-nosed brat or his scummy family is going to say anything. Now let's go and do some rounds in the neighborhoods of the true citizens of our great country. It sure makes you feel good to patrol those areas. Up on the hills of the city, a cop can even enjoy listening to the pure-bred dogs howl as we pass by their houses. Not like here in these barrios in the bowels of the city where our tires get splattered by their shit—from the dogs and the people.

* * *

The Ranch House field hands got tired of waiting for Clemente Furia Jr. They were so desperate from being on the verge of starvation that they would cook up the roots of any weeds they found. With high hopes, sitting on the wooden floors of the house, some of the workers would go to chewing on the vegetable guts as if they were warped sausages. Others, sitting on a log outside, would savor cups of the brackish root tea, enjoying it as if they were taking afternoon tea in some Parisian café.

By midnight every one of them had a horrible case of the runs. It was like they had done some type of cleanse of their digestive system, because the only thing they were shitting was dirty water.

Another day they spent sleeping to try to take their minds of their damned hunger. They would sleep for a while and then they would toss and turn in a tormented state, unable to drop off.

At night they would turn on the television. All of the field hands would crouch close to the little 12-inch screen that projected images in black and white. The majority of the commercials began to be a delectable torture for the workers' growling stomachs. They were fabulous commercials that ran in black and white on the empty screen of the workers' bellies. Their starving guts savored those succulent dishes. Their saliva dripped into a sea of spit collecting on the rotten wood making up the floor of the house. Their eyes and hands ached to reach into the screen and grab the hamburgers, the pizzas, the burritos, the cold drinks in the hands of beautiful models, the endless chips, and really anything that even resembled food.

Some of them started yelling to turn of the TV, and others said no. A few didn't want to keep on seeing the nerve-racking images of snacks and meals, but at the same time they did. It was like they were a group of kids in grade school who were watching something forbidden. The tiny black and white screen, from one second to the next, would fill up with virtual images of grocery products. Some of the workers wanted even to lick the reflections on the screen, and others wanted to bite into them like they were bodies in a pornographic movie. One of the guys started hallucinating. He was yelling for his mother and telling her how hungry he was. He rubbed at his empty stomach. His buddies started slapping him so he would shut up, but he just fell further into a sort of euphoria.

"Ay, mamacita, mamacita! I'm so hungry! Ay, ay, ay, turn off the TV! Turn it off! Turn off that fucking thing! Beat the shit out of it, so it stops, that damned malicious beast of a food fest!"

"Shut up, fucking bastard. You act like you're jerking off."

"Turn the channel before this asshole goes crazy."

Somebody, with a whack, managed to change the channel on the television. It went to a program reporting on a Hot Dog eating competition.

"Good afternoon, ladies and gentlemen! We are coming to you from Los Angeles, California, to give you a close-up of the yearly battle that takes place every October 3rd. The Hot Dog race is getting more and more popular, and more than anything it's gaining in popularity because of the five thousand dollars that any one of the participants can win. This competition is sponsored by our country's already famous producers of buns, hot dogs, ketchup and mustard. Friends, this is nothing more and nothing less than the battle that will decide who–man or woman–is the biggest hot dog eater in the United States. The race is not to see who can sell more, or who can cook more hot dogs throughout the day, but to see who can eat more hot dogs in just ten minutes."

"Ay, ay, ay, turn off that TV, you bastards!" Turn off that twisted dog of the infernal hunger of this world! Get it out of here or I'm going to eat it alive! Ay, ay, ay…!"

"Here we can see the thirty three competitors getting ready for the wieners. Each one of the contestants weighs at least two hundred fifty pounds. We had the opportunity to speak with some of them, and they told us they had eaten light in the morning and that by this time of the afternoon they are dying of hunger. Let's listen to the comments that some of them made: 'I made the sacrifice of eating only one hamburger this morning because I want to win the five thousand dollar prize.' 'All I ate this morning was an apple, nothing else.' 'I'm going to break the national record of eating more hot dogs than any other American.' 'I think I can eat twenty or more.' 'Yep, I'm gonna put on a lot of ketchup and mustard. I might add a jalapeño, but I'm not sure at this point.'"

"Ay, ay, ay…!"

"Enough already, you sons of bitches! Don't fuck with me. Shut that dick off. This asshole is going to die on us right here. Just look how he's writhing around like he was having a baby, but full grown."

"You shut up, fucking Fly! Let me watch the TV in peace. I want to see how those people dog those Hot Dogs. This is totally cool. I've never in my life seen such a doggalicious deal."

"*This is my second time in the contest. Last year I only ate twelve Hot Dogs, but I think that today I can eat more than twelve. A lot of the contestants, after the race, we go to the bathroom and throw up the Hot Dogs, and that way we don't get a stomach ache and we can eat a lot more Hot Dogs.*"

"*Very good, ladies and gentlemen. The hot dog gobbling has begun. Look at that guy, he just stuffed an entire Hot Dog into his mouth in one bite, like the wolf did to Little Red Riding Hood's grandmother.*"

"Get out of there, you idiot, don't you know that donkey meat isn't see-through! Fuck you and your momma, asshole! Eat me! Look, look how those bastards are eating those weenies!"

"Ay, ay, ay! Turn off that TV! Turn it off! Ugh, ugh, huuugh…"

"*Just look at this lady. She sticks her hot dog in the middle of the bun, spreads on mayonnaise, ketchup, mustard, and watch out because she almost sprayed us with that enormous bite she just took out of that Hot Dog. Now watch how she takes a jalapeño, bites into it, takes a sip of water and gets ready to prepare her eighth Hot Dog! Unbelievable, truly unbelievable! Now we're standing in front of the biggest eater of them all, at least for now, because they still have a minute and thirty seconds left. He has stuffed in a total of exactly thirty Hot Dogs. In second place is this muscle-bound blond with twenty nine, and in third place with twenty seven is this woman dressed all in mustard, excuse me, I meant to say in mustard yellow…*"

"You bastards, do you see what you've done? You've gone and fucked up the flipping TV with your flipping tugs and tussles like you were a pack of dogs. And you, Fly! Go and take a flying fuck at your momma. All of you, you bastards, fuck your momma. Now who has the balls to go and bring back one of the Harrison cows?"

"Turn off the TV! Ay, ay, ay!"

"Shut up already, you idiot! The television is beat to shit thanks to you guys. It won't turn on any more."

"I'm going to go right now and bring you something to eat, you sons of bitches. Damn gang of assholes, starving to death. I swear on my mother's pussy that I'm going to bring you one of those fucking Harrison calves so we can stuff ourselves like those dogs on the television."

"They're gonna throw you in the can if they catch you, Copper. Don't go looking for it, fucking Coppie, because you'll end up all the way in Mexico. Fucking Furia will show up, and he can save our asses with some dough before you can blink."

"Calm yourself down, Copper. Calm down, dude."

"You and Furia can fuck your mothers. I'll be damned if I'm going another night without eating. You all can go ahead and die of hunger, fucking assholes! Whoever wants to come and help me, well come on ahead, and whoever doesn't want to can fuck themselves. I'm no asshole and if I get the goods, we'll all get it good."

* * *

In the barn Copper found a metal rod that he took from an old tractor, and he crept through the orchards, followed by two of his buddies. They arrived just before midnight to one of the stables of the Harrison Ranch milk cows. They crossed one set of railings, then another, and another, and finally they found themselves facing their victims, the milk cows. There were so many animals that Copper didn't know which one to crack over the head with his iron bar. Copper looked for a little calf, but in that corral he only saw mature cows. He snuck up on one of the spotted, spotted cows. Not in the least disturbed, the milk-producing animal just kept chewing her cud under the light of the full, full moon.

Copper squeezed the metal bar between his hands. The spotted cow breathed with such tranquility that he started to notice how her two huge eyes shone like two mirrors. She switched her tail and ears just a bit, timidly, at the appearance of the three barely human shadows. Copper raised the metal with both hands and felt a faint wave of compassion at the beast's sweet gaze. His stomach turned and he felt faint, but he held the iron even tighter despite his shaking knees. He remembered how hungry he was. So, since there wasn't any way out of it, he swung the steel rod down in a fierce arc right onto the middle of the spotted heifer's brow, and she instantly fell senseless.

The three assailants took out knives and a tranchete* to cut up the beef. They planned to take back great hunks of meat tied to a pole that they would carry between the three of them. Copper was the first one to pull out his blade.

"Grab its hooves, fucking Fly. Let me stick my knife into this beast."

Copper started to slice the milk cow's hide, starting at the throat and moving toward her hind feet.

"Cut out her tongue, dude. We can cook us up some really bitchin' tacos with that tongue."

"Wait just a minute, fucking Fly! Let me see. Pull it out hard so I can cut it down at the base."

They tugged on the animal's tongue, not knowing that she still was a cow and not quite beef yet. The spotted animal, who wasn't dead yet, just knocked out from being hit over the head, woke up in that moment. She leapt up running and vomiting gushes of blood, even through her nostrils. The whole herd of milk producers in the stable startled so badly that it looked like they had seen the devil himself running around on four legs. The wounded beast ran like a crazed ghost all around the corral. The three bandoliers, not far from being crazed from fright themselves, took off running past the railings.

* * *

"They're Mexicans! Let's stop them. They look very suspicious."

"A beef tongue, huh? Let's take a look. Why are you so upset and scared, and why are you running in such a hurry? Where are you going with a beef tongue at this time of night?"

"We're very hungry, Mr. Officer, sir. We're taking it to the Ranch House to cook it. Tongue tacos are absolutely delicious. Haven't you ever tried them?"

"How disgusting! You Mexicans will eat any damned shit. Maybe we should cut your tongues out so you can't talk and you can just work like burros. Like burros. You hear me? That's right, like burros."

"What should we do with them, Sergeant? They've got blood on their clothes. Should we toss them in jail on suspicion of murder? Should send them to the Border Patrol for deportation? After all, they're just a bunch of starving wetbacks."

"Very good, rookie. You're learning to love your country. Our country. The country that feeds so many illegal immigrants, and exactly for that reason they should be grateful for being fed, but most of them aren't. You are, right? I see that you love our country, in spite of the fact that your last name is… I don't mean anything by it, but you know what I'm saying, right...?"

* * *

Harrison Ranch became famous for having the best milk cow in the world. The Mute Cow, during her bovine existence, ended up traveling to various national and international competitions, and said milk cow won every single contest. There at Harrison Ranch nobody ever found out how the Mute Cow lost her tongue, and nobody ever figured out the long scar underneath her neck.

The Harrisons ordered and had erected at the ranch entrance an enormous marble statue of The Mute Cow. The milk-producing miracle appeared on television commercials publicizing all sorts of dairy products that Harrison produced.

The Mute Cow became so popular that she attracted the attention of scientists, veterinarians, and sociologists. The scientists came up with all kinds of explanations for why The Mute Cow's production of milk was so high. Some of them claimed it was the alfalfa grown in the rich land of the San Joaquin Valley, others that it was the water that the animal drank, on top of the perfect climate, which had something to do with it too. Others said this and that. In general, everybody was in agreement about the possible reasons for the phenomenon.

The Harrison veterinarians and a sociologist that they contracted to study The Mute Cow's case couldn't figure out why the dairy cow would go into a whirling frenzy every once in a while. Most of the time, The Mute Cow would chew her cud peacefully, but then without warning it was like somebody had stuck a red-hot screw into her brains, and she would take off tearing around the stable as if the bovine devil was running after her.

Walking down the halls of the dairy farm, the psychologist was chatting with Mr. Harrison and said: “Because she grew up without a tongue, we can deduce that the animal never was able to express herself freely, that is to say, she never was able to moo openly like all the normal cows. Even cows need to be able to moo freely, Mr. Harrison. It seems like it couldn’t be true, no? But when man or beast is deprived of motherly love or suffer hunger, they act like wild animals locked in a cage. The closed spaces they inhabit become filled with monsters and darkness.”

“That’s enough superstitions, my good man! Let’s cut to the chase. How much do I owe you?”

“Mr. Harrison, I’m only going to charge you what we had agreed upon, but I will continue to study the case because personally, between you and me here, I will confess that I am very interested in the Animal condition. Do you know what I mean? I was studying to be a veterinarian but then I changed majors to psychology and…”

The Harrison Ranch vets were of the opinion that it must have been a worm or a fly that made the dairy animal go so crazy. For his part, the psychologist was inclined to believe that The Mute Cow had suffered hunger and maternal neglect when she was a young heifer.

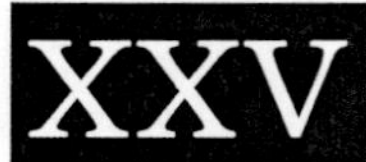

XXV

Selma

The coyote named Chita stopped at the first McDonalds that he saw along the side of Highway 5 when he got into Los Angeles. Mona went in and bought fifteen number ones for their chickens and two number sevens for her and her boss, Chita. They stuffed their faces with the hamburgers as they continued on toward their destination of Stockton, California.

"You could have ordered us a few green peppers, boss!" said one of the chicks in the group. "This salsa is too sweet and doesn't really taste like anything."

"Ha, ha, ha! That's not salsa. It's ketchup, and all of you are going to Stockton, where they make a whole shitload of that. Pretty soon y'all are going to be sending loads of dollars back home thanks to that ketchup that the white people eat so much of, and that the rich little Mexicans start to crave as well."

"Well, we'll see if we end up all ketchup-happy like the white folk," joked the girl. "They should put at least a little bit of pepper in it. Or don't white folk have hot peppers? If they don't have them, well, they can just whistle and in Mexico we can lend them all the hot peppers they want. In Mexico we're all pepper-crazy, don't you think? Of course we are. We'll lend some to the pale-faces, but on the condition that they lower that beggarly external debt that has us in the shit house."

Chita popped the last morsel of bread in his mouth and drank down half of his soft drink, then gave such an enormous burp that he started to rub his belly.

"This meal didn't cost you a penny. It was on me. I bought you lunch because you've turned out to be lucky little chickens for me. I think that the fat lady put a spell on that gringo from all the kissing and hugging she gave him. I still can't believe they didn't do anything to you."

"He could barely hold me up with both arms, what a hopeless case, and then he backed away from me so quick, like he had seen a ghost," remarked the lady in question, at which everybody busted up laughing.

At the San Clemente checkpoint, the immigration agents had received orders from higher up to give a green light to the undocumented workers. Those days, the agents were just pretending to do their job of combing the crags and bushes.

At another checkpoint outside of Bakersfield, the Border Patrol agents could see how loaded down Chita's van was, and nevertheless they didn't give him any trouble. His was one of the special journeys of human contraband that were being arranged these days. As they pulled up to the checkpoint, two agents signaled for them to go on without stopping. These were exclusive deliveries of Mexican "chicken" that the Hunt company had ordered.

In Stockton, California, the manager Richard Castro had just been recognized and rewarded by his supervisors. Thanks to him, the company's earnings had tripled over the last six years. All of this was possible because of the reduction in factory accidents, the lack of medical coverage for employees, preserving high quality and raising production levels with fewer personnel, the maintenance of minimum wage salaries, and long work-days without paying overtime. How did the devilish Richard do it? That's what he had studied business in of the top California universities for.

"Boys, if we don't have any accidents in the factory this year, you're all going to get a nice present from Santa Claus," Richard would tell his workers in the monthly general meetings. "Mexicans are strong men, real machos, and they don't start crying when they skin their knees or something, right boys?"

There were workers who had suffered serious injuries, but they put up with the backaches, sore necks, and pain in their legs hoping to receive a Christmas bonus. They never went to see a doctor, because then what would their co-workers say, or what would the ladies think? The guys who worked in loading and shipping all had coughs due to the horrid stench that drifted out of the huge containers of waste that they had under their noses all day. Like Pérez, the one with the big moustache, his wife would start flapping her jaws as soon as one of the men complained of a headache. The minute somebody so much as mentioned that they had some symptom or another, and right away the big gal would open her mouth—with its own considerable moustache—to call them all a bunch of fairies. "Tomorrow I'll bring you a headache patch."

Most of the women who worked there ended up with their feet swelling from so many hours standing on the concrete floor. By noon they all looked like storks. They blamed their shoes, their tight pantyhose, or how fat they had gotten. Rubbing alcohol, holy water, a nice beer, and home remedies from the Yerbabuena store were the only medicine that the workers in the ketchup factory had access to. You had to endure. If you even thought about going to the clinic or a hospital, you could kiss your Christmas bonus goodbye. Worse, you'd hear the familiar "the Big Boss doesn't need anybody right now" from the lips of the ass-kissing floor supervisors. In that factory you saw some serious injuries. Injuries that the workers would wear like tattoos, carrying them back from the United States to their final resting places in Mexico.

The Hunt Company had signed a new contract with three of the most popular hamburger chains in the United States. They had to up production levels. That meant more workers. Arms, arms, young arms. Richard knew how to deal with problem heads, like the workers who already had a green card. Those guys already knew that if they worked more than eight hours in a row they qualified for overtime, and they knew that if the season ended, they had the right to receive unemployment benefits.

To bring over strong young arms was only a question of a couple phone calls. The first one was made by Mr. Glenn, an immigration officer who years ago had been his roommate at Stanford University. The second call Richard Castro made himself, to one of the restaurants on the border, Kentucky Fried Gizzards.

In Chita's van everybody had finished their hamburgers and they had the luxury of burping from the soft drinks they had downed. But they had to suppress their need to let out a few farts, for fear of letting out a noisy one. All of the chickens were spaced out, lulled by the hum of the cars on the freeway. The only one that didn't drift off was the girl that kept asking questions to whoever who was listening.

"I haven't seen us pass a single toll booth yet. Don't they have toll booths here?"

"No!" Chita answered, watching her for a moment in the rear view mirror.

"Hunh! Well, these Gringos really got it going on. Man, in Mexico we would have already passed thirty toll booths I bet. They say they're private roads. That's just yarns the government spins! They invest in a highway so they can live off of the tolls. And let everybody fend for themselves. Let the poor folk crack their skulls wide open knocking into each other, from all the holes in the free highways, but whatcha gonna do?"

Chita turned on the radio and tuned it in to Radio Campesina.

"Radio Campesina, the station by the people and for the people! Turn up your radio, so even our Mexican chickens can hear it! We send out greetings to everybody from Jalisco, Michoacán, and the whole Republic!"

"Yee-hah! Hey there radio guy, wouldn't you know it, I'm Jaliscan from my head to my toes!"

"Que se me acabe la vida, frente a una copa de vino…"[9] The announcer interrupted the song to give a yell. "It almost makes me want to go *backward* to the old homestead, *paisanos*!"

"Watch out you don't fall down going *backward*, dummy! If it's easy enough to fall down going forward, just imagine going backward," jibed the girl, and Chita laughed at her.

The girl, good-looking and big-hipped, started to get into Chita's good graces. The Coyote told Mona to let the girl have her seat. As he drove, Chita couldn't take his eyes off of the girls breasts, hard as pewter, and her legs painted into a pair of jeans. The van was eating up the miles on the highway as Chita and the girl from the state of Jalisco were heating up the conversation.

"I used to work in Guadalajara. I worked for a jeans company called Anchor Blue."

---

9 This song by José Alfredo Jiménez starts: "Let me die looking at a glass of wine…"

"What happened? Why did you leave the gig?"

"What do you mean, leave it? Who ever told you that I left the job? Man, they fired my ass! All for having mentioned the word union."

"They fired you just for that?"

"Well, also for opening my big mouth. I told them that I was going to go on the TV show *Ocurrió Así*[10] and see if they listened to my complaints."

Chita cracked up laughing.

Chita started imagining the girl without any clothes on. Driving up and down the mountains of Los Angeles at fifty-five miles an hour, he imagined making love with her. He figured that Richard Castro would give him a nice bonus for bringing him such a sweet little wetback babe who to top it all off would work at the ketchup factory.

The girl couldn't stop thinking of escaping so she wouldn't have to pay Chita the fifteen hundred dollars she owed him for the ride through the mountains. Actually she would be paying the money to Richard Castro. The Coyote Chita was going to get six hundred dollars for each illegal he brought, and the rest of the money went to line the pockets of the kiss-ass *Chicanito*, Richard Castro.

They stopped in another McDonalds, and the girl really wanted to take off running, but where to? She felt like she was living in a fantasy world. She saw cars with their headlights on in the middle of the day, drivers talking on their cell phones, accidents, ambulance sirens blaring, lights on cop cars whirling, drivers pinching and slapping themselves so they wouldn't fall asleep on the road. Those highways with bridges so long that they reminded her of hog intestines filled with cement, making the McDonald's hamburger churn and upset her stomach.

Coming into the San Joaquin Valley you started to see vineyards, and the freeway looked like it was tattooed with red cars. The young woman for just a moment felt like jumping out of the van. Just like that, at full speed, but then a more intelligent idea occurred to her.

---

10 *Ocurrió Así*, literally "That's How it Happened," is a program of breaking news in the style of *Dateline*.

"Hey you, I really need to go to the bathroom. Why don't you pull over?"

"Why not?"

Chita stopped on the side of the freeway. The girl had to pee behind a tree.

"Hey, why don't you let me pee in peace? Go away, go over there!"

"You're crazy. You think I'm going to leave you alone?"

Chita turned his back on her and acted like he couldn't see a thing. He didn't give the men permission to come out at all, afraid that his chickens would turn into hares. The girl got back up into the van making a face. She still wanted to run off through the rows of grapevines.

When they were passing through Bakersfield the girl started needing to take a dump. She decided to hold it because she was embarrassed for Chita to see her do it. She thought that Chita would make her shit beside a tree and then he would walk over and hand her a McDonald's napkin to wipe herself.

They arrived in the city of Selma to fill up with gas. The girl got all excited when she saw a billboard saying "Welcome to Selma."

"Selma!" voiced the girl. "Ah, shoot! I thought the sign said Selma Rodriguez."

"What's up?" asked Chita. "This is Selma, the city of raisins."

Selma Rodriguez was the name of the girl, and she already had made up her mind to stay in Selma if she got the chance.

Chita went to pay for the gas up in the Texaco office. Mona took the van's gas cap off and then put the keys back into the ignition.

Selma took the wheel and started the motor. Mona didn't have time even to yell because he ended up knocked to the ground from Selma's violent take-off. Mona got up whistling and yelling insults.

"What in the hell happened, dude?" Chita asked Mona. "Who took the van, you jerk?"

"That woman. The fucking woman."

"I thought you were a jerk, but you're an idiot!" And he gave Mona a good kick in his rear.

Selma went down a road that took her among the vineyards. She turned down a series of dirt roads, and she didn't get further than ten miles before she ran out of gas.

"Get out, you idiots! Let's get out of her, because we are free. We don't have to pay a red cent to that bastard thief Chita or the so-called Richard the shit who they say was going to be our boss. Without a doubt he was going to be a son of a bitch."

They disappeared into the vineyards. Two of the young men kept on Selma's tail, running after her until they arrived at a vineyard where some field hands were on the job.

Back at the Texaco station, Chita—who could get by in English—was answering the police officers' questions. The police report said that his vehicle had been stolen.

"Call your insurance, buddy."

"Bunch of good for nothing bastards. Insurance, my ass, I don't even have any! I'm sure that an insurance company would fork out money when my chickens steal the van," all of which he did not say to the police when it ran through his head.

"You teasing bitch! I should have fucked you last night. If I find you I'm going to kill you, you bitch of a bigger bitch."

Selma and the two young men who were with her walked up to a group of workers and asked the foreman for a job.

"Excuse me sir, those guys over there told us that you are the foreman here, and we are looking for work. Look, this here is Melitón, and this one is…"

"Enough already! You don't have to introduce them all to me like they were a bunch of fifteen year-old debutantes. Have you worked doing paper trays before?"

"Trays? Well, if you call those papers with those things that look like flies 'trays', well, I don't think so, right, Felimón and Melitón?"

"Stop fucking around! Do you know how to turn trays or not?"

"Well, the truth of the matter is that we don't know how boss. But if you tell us how, we'll get right at it."

"That's fine. Why are you all so sweaty?"

"Oh, that. It's just that every morning we go out to do exercise, but since we really need a job right now, we decided to go running in this direction so we could ask the foreman for work, and that's you."

The foreman Clemente Furia Jr. noticed something strange about the three friends, but he decided to give them work with the trays because he was under contract and he wanted to finish gathering the raisins as soon as possible. Also, Selma really caught his eye. Her tight jeans showed off her nice figure.

He assigned the new workers a furrow and gave them some sheets of paper so that they could jot down at the end of the furrow how many trays they had turned. When Selma got to the end of her first furrow she had turned 350 trays. On one of the sheets of paper she wrote in large letters, THREE HUNDRED FIFTY TRAYS TURNED BY SELMA RODRIGUEZ.

"What is your name?"

"My first name is Selma and my last name is Rodriguez."

"Don't fuck with me, bitch. I didn't ask you the name of this shithole of a town."

"I assure you, Mr. Foreman, that my first name is Selma and my last name is Rodriguez."

Clemente Furia Jr. kicked at the roll of raisins where Selma had written the number of her trays and her name.

"From here on out your name is going to be Sor Juana Inés."[11]

---

11 The most famous of all Mexican women poets, Sor Juana Inés de la Cruz wrote during the time of the colonization of Mexico. Orozco is the muralist, Paz the well-known philosopher, Revueltas a novelist, and Buendía a character from Colombian Gabriel García Márquez's novel *One Hundred Years of Solitude*.

Selma didn't understand why the foreman was changing her name. Without making a peep, looking at the ground, she walked over to the next furrow. Selma realized that all of her fellow workers had borrowed names. One was called Clemente Orozco, others Octavio Paz and José Revueltas. Clemente Furia Jr. chose names for his workers from the atheist monk Mateo's books.

The foreman, in addition to giving them names of famous writers, painters, or characters from novels, invented their social security numbers. The white folk didn't care or acted like they didn't know. Melitón was christened with the name José Arcadio Buendía.

The three newcomers finished the workday practically on their knees, when at six o'clock in the evening they returned to the Ranch House.

Selma didn't even feel like washing up and lay down like Christ on the cross on the wooden floor of the house. At eight in the evening she woke up with a fever and hungrier than a stray dog. A decent guy, Melitón, who barely could walk from the rash on his butt, offered Selma a taco with beans and potatoes.

"Don't you dare give me any ketchup or I'll tell your momma on you," she told her good friend, who flirting gave her a jalapeño.

Selma, California is the world capital of raisins. It is in the middle of grape country. Grapes made into raisins that are sent to other continents. Wrinkled raisins decorating the pastries served daily in the White House in Washington, D.C. Raisins hammered by the President and all of his cabinet at lunch time.

Mother Selma, I am the raisin. I am the sweat of your wine. Pray for us, the downtrodden and sad of face. Pray for all of us who cry in the dark for fear of being called chickens.

In the morning the three new workers couldn't even get up, they woke up hurting so badly, but Clemente Furia Jr. got them up with a combination of horn honking and cursing. They didn't even have time to run over to the orchard to relieve themselves, so off they went to the trays with their stomach full of trash.

Selma really needed to go to the bathroom and she immediately asked Gertrudis where they were. Gertrudis laughed at how naïve Selma was and pointed her finger toward the sea of vines. Selma went into the vines to relieve herself and when she unfastened her pants she realized that she couldn't squat down. Gertrudis came over and told her that this is how it is for the first few days, and that she would have to go standing up. Selma couldn't hold off anymore so she let go in front to pee and squeezed as hard as she could in back so nothing would come out there.

Selma was sorry she had ended up in this precise shithole of a town. Inside she raged and cursed her namesake, Selma, California.

"Selma you bastard. Fucking bitch. Selma you whore. Fuck you, your mother, and your fucking grapes."

By noon they had finished turning the trays and they went on to pick them all up. The John Deere tractor was driven by Clemente Furia Jr. He aligned it in the furrow where Selma was picking up the rolls of raisins. Selma, awash in a sea of sweat, bent over to pick up the rolls of raisins, then ran to empty them in the boxes. Selma's ass was dripping wet, and Clemente Furia Jr. didn't move his eyes off her backside. Furia sped up the tractor more and more, and Selma picked up the rolls more hurriedly. She dashed to empty the packets of raisins. She impaled the emptied sheets of paper on a rod soldered onto the front of the tractor. Selma bent down and Furia sped up. Selma, each time she bent over, felt like what the foreman wanted was to give her a few pokes from behind with his oversized iron rod.

Selma moved as quickly as she could, but the machine seemed like it was possessed. Selma started seeing stars. She couldn't keep up any longer with the accelerated pace of the tractor and they young woman fell to her knees onto the loose earth. Maria helped her get up. She dabbed water on her forehead. She started to feel a little better. Her jeans were drenched in blood. Leaning back underneath the vines, she came back around somewhat, but the blood kept on coursing from between her legs.

"Selma! What were you thinking, getting your period at a time like this. You have to learn to control your period, so it only comes on your days off."

"God, sister, lend me a pad."

"A what?"

"A feminine napkin."

"You wish, even if it was just paper napkins. I don't have anything. I'll go right now and look for something up in the van."

Selma stayed where she was, flopped down under the vines as if she had been crucified to the earth. From the ground she saw the rolls of raisins and with all her heart wished she could used one of those rolls as a pad. She thought that one of those big fat tamales would absorb all of the wine that was running between her legs. Almost on all fours, she took a piece of paper off of the ground. She shook it, tore it, and started shaping it into the form of a feminine napkin. Along the edge she inserted a length of vine and in the center, for absorption, she put leaves and raisins. Maria helped Selma stick the raisin tamale underneath her purple panties.

"Whore Selma bitch! Bitch, daughter of the biggest whore in town!" that evening in Stockton, the Coyote named Chita growled with rage.

That same night, in the Ranch House, under the full August moon, turned into a wild animal, before spraying herself down, Selma shook all the raisins from her sex.

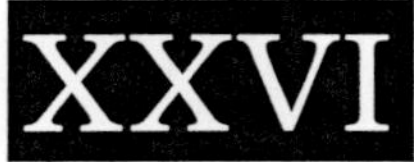

At the Belly Button of the Tijuana Hills

At the belly button of the hills between Mexico and the United States, Macaria, losing blood, stayed prone with her legs apart. The Coyote and his chickens disappeared like ghosts in the darkness of night when they heard the dogs' barking and the voices in English of the Border Patrol.

Macaria had not meant to cross the border on her own. She was crossing the border with Coyote and the other wetbacks or barbed wire boys. The other wetbacks might still be crossing the border on their own, but she, Macaria, couldn't. Macaria wasn't alone. Macaria was with her baby. Crawling they passed underneath a tunnel. Dragging themselves they hid among some bushes. Trotting they got all the way to a barbed wire fence. Macaria hugged her belly with all her strength, as if to keep the little life she held in her womb from slipping away.

She stood there looking at the barbed wire that divided the two countries. The rest of them had gotten scared and run when they heard the noise coming from the other side, but not her. Macaria, sobbing, just stared at the barbed wire fence. The border that divided the two countries had been turned into quite the clothesline where the winds coming from north and south would hang things onto the metal barbs. It had blown women's panties and slips up onto the barbed wire. Macaria figured that her underwear was probably still up there from when she lost it nine months ago. A Coyote had raped her. Her boyfriend Clemente Furia found her weeping, tossed into the brush. He took her by the arm, and together they found the courage to cross the border. They got to California, but before she gave birth she was deported from a garlic field where she was working beside Clemente Furia.

Macaria kept on gazing, perplexed, at the clothesline border, covered with hats, handkerchiefs, panties, diapers, baby clothes, trash. Macaria untied a pair of baby shoes and held them to her stomach. She took down a little piece of stained blanket. She felt a cramp grab her belly.

In the distance she heard the Coyote calling her to come back. On the other side she heard the barking of the dogs grow closer and closer. Through the night sky passed a helicopter policing the border. Macaria tried to dig a hole in the earth with her hands so she could cross under the fence. She already was feeling the labor pains. In a manner of seconds her baby boy would be born. The nationality of her child depended totally on her. She badly wanted to get to the United States to give birth, but her son didn't give her enough time. Underneath the fence, smack dab in the middle of the border, at the belly button of the hills, she gave birth to Clemente Furia Jr. The dogs of the Border Patrol agents came sniffing to the place she had her baby, but Macaria had already picked up her baby and left the birthing site. The dogs entertained themselves beneath the moon, gulping down blood clots and fragments of the umbilical cord that had joined Macaria Mendoza and her son Clemente Furia.

XXVII

Col and Cara

We did everything we could to take Cara's body to his land, but we couldn't do it, Clown," wrote Mateo on these pages. "I managed to get in touch with his cousin, the one that lived in Los Angeles, the one they supposedly called Col. He was able to get a hold of two of his uncles on the phone, but it didn't help at all. We did everything we could do and we weren't able to send his body to his hometown, Rancho de Guadalupe. Col sold his black car, and even that wasn't enough to get his cousin Cara a decent burial with his people.

"Col stayed here at the Ranch House drinking wine for two weeks straight to try to put out the flames of agony he felt for his cousin. One day that bastard Clemente Furia Jr. came in and ran him off, kicking him in the ass. During the days Col was here, he told me a lot of stories."

"I remember how after Cara's burial, I went to a vineyard to get a few sheets of wrapping paper. It was the paper that we laid out along the furrows to dry out the grapes into raisins. I brought back a handful of pages and sat down to write the story of how Col and Cara got the idea of coming to the United States to earn dollars. Clown, do you remember how you used to like me to read you the story about Col and Cara? You always would fall asleep before I finished reading it, and half asleep you would laugh at the part about Brother Matalote.

"Cara, look at my little boat, how the current catches it. This one is going to make it to the other side for sure," Col told his cousin excitedly.

"I don't think so. Look, there's a lot of algae over there, and it's going to get caught!"

"Lets take some algae home for Mama Lola's chickens!" Col and Cara yelled with enthusiasm.

Clown, you didn't know it, but Col and Cara were first cousins and they had been born on the same day. From when they were very little they were inseparable friends. Col was thin, dark, with big black eyes. He was so skinny that he could slip through any set of bars like a cat. Cara was fat and blonde, and you hardly noticed his light blue eyes in that big round face.

The cousins set themselves to gathering algae out of the Pantoja family gorge. The algae looked like a green cloud that floated on the surface of the water, lain out so it looked like the states of some country. These canals had been built by the Pantojas to irrigate their plots of land that were close to the Lerma River zones, the Repartidor and the Potrero up above, which were the most difficult to water. Col, the braver and crazier of the two when it came to mischief or adventure, rolled up his sleeves before sticking his arm in the water. Col thrashed about with his hands trying to reach the algae. As hard as he tried, he couldn't even shoo off the bees or butterflies that flew around above the algae from sunup to sundown. It seemed like the insects' job was to kiss each one of the little green wheels that rose up from the water.

Cara, a little desperate, dug mud up from the shore and rolled it into round balls with his hands. He grabbed the mud balls with both hands and heaved them into the water, making pools where many of the bees and butterflies drowned. The impact of the balls splashed out dozens of snails. Some of the snails with a little luck fell onto the thistles growing along the sides of the canal. Others with no luck at all fell like kernels of corn onto the ground, and the birds took care of them.

Col rolled his sleeves up again, but the algae was further away than it looked. Col ended up taking off his shirt and pants, until he was standing completely naked in the canal. With his body, Col broke the green cloud floating on the canal water. Now he had all the green algae he wanted right where he could reach it. When he tried to grab it, it slipped through his fingers because the cover wasn't very dense yet.

"Cara, find me something to gather it with," yelled Col.

Cara went looking for a stick or whatever might be useful in gathering the algae. He ran over to a pile of stubble that was on one of the plots. He took out a dried cane from the heap of sticks and carried it over to Col, who was waiting for him in the middle of the canal. When Cara tried to pass it to him, he lost his balance and fell, completely breaking up the green cloud.

They waited a long time before the water calmed and the green cloud started to form again. The boys began to caress the algae with the outside of the hollow bamboo. Little by little they pulled the algae toward one side of the canal, and after a long struggle they had managed to wrap some three kilos of bright green algae in Col's shirt, to give to Mama Lola's hungry chickens. They had wanted to fill even the sleeves of the shirt, but they were worn out and starving. They wanted to go home to eat, rest, and get ready for the party that their town celebrated every December.

The music, the fireworks, and the church bells could be heard even on the outskirts of the town. Hearing the cheer of the village, Col and Cara began to swell with pleasure, and their hearts started to beat like a finely tuned locomotive. The town's band, on wind instruments, was playing in the gazebo as was customary every December 12. Col and Cara were walking along the main street of the town. The street was seeded with North American cars of all colors, just like every year during the town's Christmas festivities. Col and Cara said that each car was like a little gazebo stage because you heard music coming out of all of them. They approached the cars, trying to make out the names on the plates.

Col and Cara were in the habit of reading any words that they saw around them. They already knew by heart the signs that were hung on the whitewashed adobe walls around their village. There weren't a lot of signs on the walls, but the few that existed were repeated a lot. In capital letters PRI, PAN, PPS, PRD, and PDM stood out boldly on the painted adobe.[12] All of the signs had three capital letters and all of them started with the letter P. Col and Cara gave different interpretations to each of the letters and they never agreed. The only thing that they agreed on was the first letter, and they always said that it was P for poor. For them, the letters on the cars were awfully strange. Those letters weren't anything like the ones that shone on the iron plaque that the town gazebo had. The plaque on the gazebo said, *Rancho de Guadalupe Gazebo 1963*. Col

---

12 All refer to Mexican political parties, or *partidos*, hence beginning with P.

and Cara pronounced very well the words that were on that gazebo plaque, but they stumbled and stuttered reading the plates on the gazebo-cars, as they called them.

"Ne-her-se-y," said Cara.

"Neherse, stupid," Col corrected Cara.

"Col, look at that red one, it's from chingón," yelled Cara.

"Wachintón, dummy! You don't know anything."

Those names on the license plates seemed very odd to Col and Cara. The music in English coming from the cars was even weirder and stranger to them. Col and Cara continued down the main street until they ran into a group of young men who were drinking beer in front of the store run by Rosa, the one that owned the Town Mill. Col and Cara were fascinated by the young men's conversation, which they listened to, mesmerized.

"Pass me one of those birrias, ése," said one of the boys in the group.

"Hey, loco, you want another one?" a boy asked Peter.

"*Sokay ése*, I'm already suave. I'm gonna go over and *güachar the rucas*. I'll see you *al ratón*, locos," said Peter as he combed back his hair, slick with gel.

"*Calmao ése*, we'll get on with it *al rato*, after all, the only thing this *pinche pueblo* has enough of are *mulas* that can wet our whistle," ordered Jessie.

"Hey Brother Matalote, come over here!" Jessie yelled to one of the town characters. Brother Matalote was about thirty-five years old and earned a living as a peon at Rancho Guadalupe. Brother Matalote was coming to play his guitar at the only Protestant church that the town had. His nickname had nothing to do with his physical appearance, because he was tall, strong, and moreover was tireless wielding a shovel or machete on somebody's land. The Brother approached the group of young men and greeted them very agreeably.

"Good afternoon, boys! How are you? What a miracle to see you hanging out here, guys,"

"*Pinche* Brother, it's a miracle what my Z-28 can do when I stamp the gas pedal to the floor," one of the youths said to the Brother, laughing sarcastically.

"*Ése* Brother, drink one down to quench your thirst!" another young man said, offering the Brother a beer.

"Thanks a lot, boys, I appreciate it, but I can't right now," responded the Brother, laying his arm across the shoulder of one of the men, whom he asked:

"You're the one they named Chuyillo, you're the son of my godfather Jesús, who grows tomatoes, aren't you?"

"*Simón, ése*, but don't call me Chuyillo. Call me Jessie."

"Sure, that's fine. Whatever you say. Wow, you're already all grown up now, and when you left you were just a kid," Brother Matalote said humbly to Jessie.

"Yeah, pues, but you know how it goes. Here, drink a *chela* with me."

"No, I really can't right now, you see."

"Pinche Brother, don't be that way wit' me. If you want five or six cases, whatever you want. Look, after all right here I got *lana* to spare," said Jessie, showing him a fistful of dollars.

"No, I'm not saying anything. I'm just telling you the truth, that I can't drink," repeated the Brother.

"In that case, *échate* a few song here *pa' todos los camarones*," Jessie commanded.

Clearly against his wishes, the Brother sang them "El Rey" and "Paso del Norte."

"Hey, *vatos*, bring out some tips for the Brother," Jessie instructed his friends, who started to pull out dollar bills. They threw them on to the floor. Jessie gathered them up and handed them to the Brother. Brother Matalote took them unwillingly and walked away looking like he had just sold his soul to the devil. The expression on Brother's face said that he hoped to never run into that group of boys again as long as he lived.

Col and Cara were hidden behind a light post. The two cousins were cracking up laughing from seeing Brother Matalote running off.

"What in the hell are you carrying there, *locos*?" Jessie asked, walking over to Col and Cara.

"Algae for the hens," replied Col.

"*Pinches vatos*, give them corn feed."

"Oh no, cuz it's way too expensive!" responded Col, placing the shirt filled with algae on top of his head. Jessie came over to Col and with one kick sent flying the bundle that Col had on his head. All the algae fell, strewn all over the cobblestones of the street. Jessie, kicking at the algae, lost his balance. When he fell he broke some beer bottles.

"You're going to hear from my brother, stupid idiot," Col said to Jessie, crying and full of rage.

"And you're gonna have to pay for these bottles that you broke, because the man from Carta charges me for them," said Rosa, who had come out right away when she heard the sound of the broken bottles.

"How much do the sonovabitches cost? You just say how much, and *ya se acabó el pedo*. I've got enough to pay for your whole damn shack," Jessie told the owner. Jessie paid her for the bottles, and he tossed Col and Cara a bill so they could go buy some candy.

That night, Col and Cara sat down on the curb to eat peanuts. The two cousins admired the youths who came in their cars from the United States. Both of them said that as soon as they grew up, they would go to El Norte and earn a lot of dollars so they could buy a brand-new car.

Col and Cara looked closely and saw that among the algae were scads of snails. The ladies were starting to take down their booths. The cars were starting to leave, pealing out and burning rubber on the cobblestones. The wind started to play with the peanut shells thrown into the streets. Col and Cara stayed sitting there watching the snails that were on the stones, moving toward the outskirts of the town. Col and Cara, surprised, imagined that the snails knew the road back to the canal where the boys had brought them from. They thought that maybe the snails could scent to aroma of the canal water, and that's why they were moving without deviation in that direction. Perplexed, the two cousins asked themselves how long it would take them to get back to that green cloud floating on the surface of the canal water at the Pantoja place. They wondered if when they got to their destination, whether they would remember the town and come back.

What a long journey those snails must have made to get to where they were going. Fifteen years later, Col and Cara were inside a black car with California plates. They were parked in from of the store run by Rosa from Molino, drinking a few beers.

"Good afternoon boys. How are you? Wow, look at that car you have!" Brother Matalote said to them as he passed by riding his burro, but he didn't hear anything they might have said in return, because his burro was in a hurry.

"And who is that güey?" asked Col.

"I bet his momma knows," replied Cara.

"Get that rola rollin'" ordered Col, already halfway drunk. "Rosaaaa... Give us a couple more."

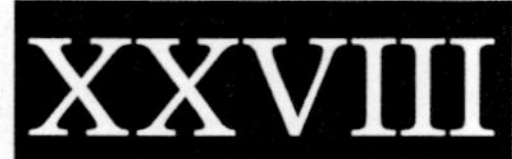

XXVIII

The Strikers

Clemente Furia Jr. came to get his workers at the Ranch House at seven o'clock at night to take them to plant peach saplings, King of Diamonds. It was not the workers' usual schedule, but circumstances forced them to labor at night as if they were hunting frogs. It was going on two weeks that the Ranch House workforce had been planting baby trees at night on account of the fact that during the day the strikers were haunting the fields of the San Joaquin Valley, asking the field workers to join them in the union cause under their leader César Chávez.

"Mother fucking strikers sons of bitches! It's their fault we have to work all fucking night like a bunch of street whores!" yelled Clemente Furia Jr., infuriated, as he adjusted the light on his miner's hard hat. "Fucking shit of a Monk! That son of a dickhead, it's his fault too. I'm sure he's going around arm in arm with the strikers, and I have no doubt that he's the one who got them looking at us. Fucking dogs! All they do all day is screw around, yelling and screaming with their flags with eagles and the fucking Virgin. They're a gang of bastards that want to take away my foreman job so that they can have it themselves. Fucking strikers, sons of bitches, gang of limp dicks! And what's up with y'all? What are you doing staring at me like a bunch of idiots? Get the lead out! Put on those helmets and turn on the lights and let's go hunt some frogs. Ha, ha, ha!"

The workers picked up their shovels, picks, and lighted helmets as if they were going to work in the mines. With a tilt of the head they shone the lights from their helmets on the spots marked in white, and there they struck the pickaxes to start the holes. They dug holes a half meter wide, and then out of a trailer that Furia pulled behind a tractor, they grabbed the saplings and planted them in the ground.

"Let's get the hell out of here, it's already seven in the morning, and those whoredog strikers are going to get here any minute. Bastards, they're eating our dust now! We're the early birds getting the worms. Ha, ha, ha! You, fucking Little Clown, I don't want to see you talking to that fucking Atheist Monk or I'm going to run you the hell off from the Ranch House. I already heard that he's teaching you to reading those fucking Marxist books of his. Don't believe a word that guy says, because what he's going to want you to do is to join up with him and those *sanababiche* strikers. You're gonna be sorry if you listen to that idiot. If you leave the Ranch House, I don't want you to cross my path ever again, do you hear me?"

"Yes."

"Yes what, you bastard? Listen up all of you, if you see that Atheist Monk, you tell him that I don't want him setting foot in the Ranch House from this moment forward, because if I see him I'm gonna knock his fucking head off. Those damned strikers already bought him a motorcycle so he can ride all around tossing out those fucking propaganda sheets from César Chávez and his union. Idiots! They don't even get it that field workers don't know how to read. Communists, Marxists, son of street whoredog bitches."

In the morning, in Clement Furia Jr.'s van, the workers were already on their way back to the Ranch House when they ran into the César Chávez crowd that was walking along shouting, in chorus, untiringly, throughout the country to invite the field hands to join them to support the strike.

"*El pueblo, unido, jamás será vencido*! The people, united, will never be divided! The people, united will never be divided! The people, united, will never be divided!"

"Fellow workers, our brothers, we ask you to abandon your labors and come join us in the cause. We are demanding our rights. The ranchers will keep on ignoring us if we don't give them an ultimatum. We demand better working conditions for all the workers in the fields. We can't go on living in shacks infested by roaches and rats. We demand an 8-hour work day, portable toilets, clean water."

They looked like the swarm of a beehive walking along the edge of the fields and roads. The hive of strikers just got bigger and bigger, as they moved from field to field.

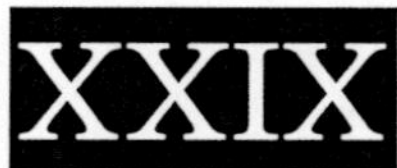

The Power of the Word

"What are you doing?" Little Clown asked Mateo, the Atheist Monk.

"I'm writing. Can't you see?" responded Mateo.

"What are you writing?"

"I'm writing everything that goes through my five senses."

"Everything?"

"Yes."

"Can you teach me to do that?"

"Do you know how to write?"

"No."

"Do you know how to read?"

"No."

"How many years did you go to school?'

"I didn't go to school."

"Wasn't there a school in your town?"

"Yes, we had one that went up to third grade. I didn't go to school because I had to take care of the goats and cows of one of the rich men in our town. The money he paid me, I gave it to my mom so she could buy salt and lard at the town store, the Conasupo."

"The we'll have to start from nothing. Like they say, you've got to begin with the letter 'o.'"

"What do those letters say?"

"What you just finished telling me. It says: Little Clown doesn't know how to read or write on account of he never went to the school in his town because he had to take care of cows and goats for a rich man in his town. The money that he was paid for taking care of goats and cows he would give to his mother so she could buy salt and lard at the Conasupo."

"The letters say what I speak?"

"The letters say what we speak, and also what we think, feel, and dream."

"How is that possible? Can you read minds?"

"No. I can't read minds, but the art of writing has magical powers."

"So I suppose you can write down everything that I have up here in my head?"

"I sure can."

"So, let's see, last night, what was I thinking about while we were planting trees?"

"You were thinking that you would like to leave the Ranch House. You have to get away from the Ranch House, Little Clown. You were imagining yourself studying in a school here in this country. Get out and start going to school, Little Clown. You imagined owning all of this land. This land is your land. Our land. Land of our ancestors, Little Clown."

"Don't go and tell Furia that I really feel like leaving the Ranch House. I don't want him to know that, please. And don't tell Selma that yesterday I imagined her without any clothes on. In my imagination I touched her wet little spider with my fingertips and she was letting me..."

"Don't worry. I didn't write down the part about Selma."

"That's great, thanks!"

"Words are powerful, like weapons, Little Clown. Words are ideas and ideas are words. A poet once said that trenches made of ideas are better than trenches made of stones."

"And is it true?"

"It's true. Damned true, by god. You've got to get out of here, Little Clown. Go! You have to learn the magical power of words. Leave!"

"And go where?"

"Far away from here."

"How?"

"Through the power of writing."

"But I don't know how to read or write. It's like I was blind. Do you see those sacks over there? I know that one of them is sugar and the other is salt. How do I know? I had to taste them with my tongue, because the letters don't mean anything to me."

"You have to leave the Ranch House, Little Clown."

"I don't know anything about the city and I don't have any relatives there. I wouldn't be able to go. I don't want to leave the country. I come from the land. I just can't see myself doing city work. I love the earth. My grandfather would say that working with the earth is the purest of all work."

"That's true. But the conditions in which the field hands work and live make it all dirty."

"My grandfather taught me to love the land. He used to say that a man who doesn't love the earth in his lifetime won't appreciate death. He would say that the earth hears and feels everything. He would tell me, 'Talk to the earth, my son. Touch her. Feel her. Lean your ear down to the ground and listen to her song. You have to love her because in the end that's where all of us are going to end up.'"

"Write!" Write down what you are telling me now."

"I already told you that I don't know how to write."

"But you can learn! You should learn about the power of writing and then come back and write your own history, my history, the history of all of us."

"How? I don't know what to do to get away from the Ranch House."

"The journey starts from the inside out. You can't tell me that you don't already imagine yourself studying in a school."

"Yes."

"So you already have begun the journey. Let's start your lessons right now. Close your eyes, and repeat after me: I exist…"

"I exist…"

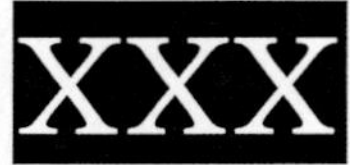

I Am the Border

"What are you doing, Little Clown?"

"I'm writing a cuícatl."

"What are you writing?"

"A cuícatl."

"What in the hell is that?"

"It's a dialogue with my heart."

"A what?"

"A poem. I'm writing poetry, look. I already wrote all of these verses."

"Poetry? What kind of son of a bitching thing is that?"

"Poetry is beautiful poems. Look, this is a poem that I have entitled "I Am the Border."

"Now you're just like the Atheist Monk. You hang around writing stuff from the Devil. Poetry? It sounds to me like things straight from Hell, to tell the God's honest truth."

"No doubt."

"And why do you write those fucking things anyway? What are they good for?"

"To express what I see, what I feel, what I think, what I dream, and to express what others feel, think, and dream."

"Don't fuck with me! So now I suppose you're a mind reader. That crazy Atheist Monk is rubbing off on you, huh? Hey guys! Guys! Come over here! Come one! Little Clown is a fortune-teller. He can see the future like that Ramayá that advertises on the radio. Sure as shitting that crazy bastard the Atheist Monk is rubbing the hell off on you. What do you think, guys? Little Clown can read our minds."

"No. I can't read minds. Knowing how to write is worth more than knowing how to read somebody's mind. Writing is poetry and poetry is writing. Poetry is saying things in a different way. It's like saying things inside out."

"You are screwed, Little Clown! What are you smoking?"

"Poetry. I'm smoking poetry. Look at this other poem I wrote the other night. It was inspired by the mole that Selma has right by her lips. Her mole isn't a mole, it's a drop of wine..."

"Come on... Get out of here and go to hell! Tell your little stories to somebody stupider than we are. I'd send that fucking poetry to the firing squad. I'll take that fucking old lady poetry and give it to her good and not even pay her. Let's see, let's see, like the blind man said! You, the great poet who can pull poetry out of your ass, make me a jacket without pulling down my pants! Look, I'm going to put it to you real simple here. I'm going to let out a big fart, and I want to see if that fucking old lady that you talk about so much can grab it and paint it red. What do you think about that? Do you think she can do it? Yes or no?"

All of the workers started laughing themselves silly and making fun of Little Clown. Little Clown, straight faced, stood up and bowed to the four directions of the earth and yelled in a hollow, echoing voice: *Tihuí, Tihuí, Tihuí, Tihuí.* Then he knelt down and gazed up at the sky as if her were giving thanks to the sun. All the workers from the Ranch House swarmed around to listen to Little Clown. Little Clown sat down cross-legged in front of his roommates and eyed closed, started to recite with feeling. With his poet's voice he gave all the workers goose bumps right away and had them totally dumbfounded from beginning to end.

I am the North. I am Death. I am the direction of earth. In this direction all that is impossible becomes possible: the pilgrims' long walks have not yet ended. All the humble descendents of Tonantzin search for me and come to me. They come to me like bees come to their hive. They are a swarm of bees, Tonantzin! I beg you Tonantzin, do not leave them helpless in this desert of bitterness.

There on the other side, in the belly button of the moon, children, elders, adults, married and single, leave behind their calli. The young students abandon their telpuchcalli to come to me. They are hungry, Tonantzin. Your poor children go out looking for life, but they don't even imagine that what they really find in me isn't honey, but death. They find physical death, and most times they run into what hurts even more, spiritual death. What else do they expect from me, if I myself am death, the direction of earth.

I have them here trapped, your children Tonantzin, within the claws of my rude labors. I make them believe that one day they will return to their calli with their fists full of gold, but that day never comes. How many times have you heard your children say, Tonantzin, "next year I'm going back to my land, God willing, if God gives me life and health, in December I'm going back to my village, if God helps me, in two or three years I'm going back home, this year or next, God permitting, it will happen when God and the Virgin will it, one day it will be, just first I'm gonna buy me a brand-new truck and get together with a blonde gal, and then I'm going back to my land." Ha, ha, ha, ha, ha! They live and die with hope between their lips, the poor children of Tonantzin. They live death day in, day out. They live me, step by step, sigh by sigh. I have them locked up in self-exile, the self-exile of undocumented workers. Ha, ha, ha, ha, ha!

Only the tlailotlaques don't come to me, because they are old wise men that one day returned from the land of the Mixtec to teach the wisdom of the writings of the teoamoxtli.

I am the South. I am the infinite blue of hope that flows in the blood of the lost and the hopeless in the desert. I am fertility. I am the direction of water. Tlalticpac. Tlalticpac. Tlalticpac. From here in this desert I shout; everything is transitory on this earth. I am the water that kisses the lips of the children lost among the dunes of a desert. I am the drop of water transformed into the desert rose. Only the children of Tonantzin have seen petals of water in the desert fall onto a blanket of anguishing thirst that shatters like crystal when it strikes the stone of the sea. They die of thirst in the desert. Ironically they are called wetbacks, these children of Tonantzin. Men and women of water, children of stone and water. Men and women of blue with their hopes evaporating in the mirage of a broken cloud that opens up over a city lost in the desert.

I am the East. I am the direction of fire. I am man. I am woman. I am the color of our Sun God. I am fire.

Tonantzin and Guadalupe. Guadalupe–Tonantzin, where are you both? Where is either one of you? Don't abandon your sons and daughters. Don't abandon them. Make them lift up their eyes to the horizon. Keep them safe from death and love.

A voice drowned among clouds of sand cries out to a woman he loves with all his heart, "I am the fire of your passions. Here I love you, in this land, in this instant. Deport me if you will, as you have done before. Believe me, I did not know that my man's hormones would relentlessly stalk your hips that you move like crazy when you walk nude across the sand. Where do you want me to go, My life went to hell in this land sown with evil indifference."

Ha, ha, ha! I am the East. I am only a mirage of the desert. I am the voice that speaks and says, "That's right, keep on sending medicine to the towns among the sand. Try to revive, with your hypocrisy, the dead lying in pieces in the sand. Crystal and stone are fused with a kiss just to shatter in a thousand shards in the memory of time. Love and war always go hand in hand. Because you don't love me I went to enlist in the army. Even though I was a wetback I was rejected by your country for my bad luck of having been born with flat feet. Oh, Jauja! I don't understand then why when I see you I don't walk with my feet firmly on the sand." Ha, ha, ha, I am the East. I am the poet's voice that says, "As many idiots have loved you, Jauja, as the wars that your Gods have wages in the last centuries." I am the East...

I am the West. I am the setting of the sun. I am the direction of air that comes and goes between the sky and the earth. I am the element that unites the heavens with the earth. I am invisible. I am strong. I am woman. I am a butterfly of air with wings of sand. I am the one who gives life to the kite that is kept up by the gaze of Tonantzin's children.

In the desert of Tarahumara, they wander without direction, the children of Tonantzin. Ixpapalotl, queen of the butterflies, don't abandon your flight of bronze wings.

Undocumented alien, Bracero, barbed-wired, child of Tonantzin, you remind me of Quetzacóatl. One day you escaped from your village, you crossed the river to Jauja; you married the blonde and got papers. For five years Jauja denied you residency, because the blonde is a con artist that feeds on wetbacks. Son of Tonantzin, during war time the government enlisted you in the Air Force. Up in your fighter jet you bombed I don't know how many cities of sand. Ah, son of Tonantzin! At the moment you least expected it your wings of steel fused with the war, and you fell into the desert in a thousand pieces. And Jauja, in homage of your posthumous courage, made you a citizen.

Why do I go to war, Jauja, if I already have you? Even the cruel words that your mouth has said to me I'm going to make them into poetry that never ends, because there are fools like me who love without any reason."

I am the West. I am purgatory. I take away and bring back messages from the living and the dead and even those who find themselves in limbo. The sons and daughters of Tonantzin know the cahuitl. The time has come for cahuitl, cahuitl. Tonantzin, your children are always abreast of time and the changes that come with me, the direction of the air...

I am the border in the middle of two countries. I am the Río Bravo, I am the Río Grande. I am air, earth, fire, water; I am the blood of the Wetback. I am the Wetback who is laid to waste in the desert of Jauja. I am the sand that sticks to your nude white body. I am the water that you gut and garrote in the brush bathed with sand. Come child, come! Drink my blood that is spilling out over this sand!

I am the crystal in the middle of two lovers who love each other with all their hearts. I am the impossible kiss. I am the kiss impossible. Impossible love. Love impossible. I am invisible. I am the Border that isn't seen. I am a Border of dust, or sand, of lime, of stone. I am porous...

Among all things, Jauja, what you like most is to swim. I don't understand, therefore, why there is so much hate toward this Wetback who is laid to waste by love in your desert. I am the desert that drinks up the lives of the undocumented aliens. I am the shore, I am the center, I am a strip of land, I am an idea, I am just an idea in the middle of the desert. I am the Border. I am where you put me. I exist if you want me to exist. The crystalstone, the stone and the crystal, are in all directions.

Son of four directions, I am enraged and saddened by what you tell me about the war. I still keep the newspaper where you are on the front page, like a complete hero, carrying in your arms a wounded enemy soldier. Rage and fury to know that the sergeant, after the reporter took the picture, ordered you to toss the fatally wounded soldier onto the sand, and you shot him full of holes, leaving him crumpled between your boots like a dog bleeding to death. The newspaper doesn't say that, in Jauja, but it is what your country does, and this, this is what is written by a minion kneeling at your feet.

I am the north, I am the south, I am death, I am life. I am man, I am woman. I am rain that feeds hate, I am water that engenders violence. I am the plow that splits the earth, I am air that rocks the grain of wheat, I am bread, I am sand, I am nothing. I am a strip of leather of an idea that divides land, that divides human beings by color and by sociopolitical conditions. I am cold, I am heat, I am water, I am fire, I am air, I am earth. I am sea, I am sky, I am moon, I am sun...

Jauja, you declare war on me and from my room I write you a phrase, I am the Border. You believe in war and I believe in peace. I am the Wetback that dies in the sand. Toss me a white flag in the middle of the desert so I can embrace your feet like a rain of dust. I walk barefoot and lost through a desert. I live on bread and water, the war brings lust. Today you eat more hamburgers than ever. You debut clothes the next size up every eight days. You drink colas all day long. Your voice isn't so clear now like in the days that you wanted to drink water from the desert!

I am the city in the middle of nowhere. I am a city of nothing and nobody. I am asphalt, lights, trash, cold, heat, thirst, trucks, brothels, dust, hunger, desires, exhaustion, sleep, children, old people, whores, crystal, plastic, paper, drugs, shit... I am a whore city. I am dollars, God in thee I believe and I trust. I am the peso in devaluation. I am ten for the price of one. I am one to ten. I am violence in the middle of two countries. I am a war, sand dunes, barbed wire fence, hills infested with violence, betrayal, violation, rape, death. Yes, I am tunnels, bridges, coyotes, wetbacks, chickens, barbed-wire, undocumented aliens, braceros, Hispanics, Latinos, Mexicans, Mexican-Americans, Chicanos, immigration, border patrol, agent, peace-keeping forces, Minutemen.

I am the war between two countries. They have waged war on us. In 1845 war was declared. Unjustified war. Mexico, belly button of the moon. Land of a thousand colors, perfect white to put into action a plan of Manifest Destiny. The Green Plan written by politicians to push past the boundaries until the blue land, the direction of water.

I am the sand in your desert. I am your dog that you used to love so much. I am the secret rage of a man-dog who loves you. I am the blood of the Wetback that spills out before your soldier boots. Goodbye and good riddance, Jauja. I don't owe anybody anything. I'm leaving, I owe you nothing, and I take nothing with me, only the memory of you.

What are you looking for now in my fatherland, Jauja? Your image saturates the entire country. My nation welcomes you with open arms, and there are even those who kneel down at your feet. A custom of our people, from time immemorial.

Walk naked along the beaches, swim in the sand over my grave, Jauja. Eat all you want, taste the tortillas made of blue corn. Drink all you desire, drink pulque, tequila with the worm and caña. Spread all over your white skin the clay of many colors that exists in my nation. Visit all the cities: those of stone, those underground quarries, those made of adobe, those made of glass, those made of cardboard.

Go into all the churches to see their saints and their virgins, since you don't know any more how to pray in the Christian tongue. See everything in my country. Listen to everything, smell everything, touch everything, taste everything.

One day you were surprised, Jauja, by the first beggar you ran into on the street. You saw the misery of his physical existence and you stretched out a coin. He rejected your alms. You exploded with rage, Strawberry Girl. Even in the most humble corner of my nation, we are born with pride in our hearts.

Don't forget to go skinny dipping in the sea at Blue Beach. There floating are the remains of a poet who at night in his room wrote you so many verses in the sand.

Goodbye... I am the Border... I am where you want me to be... I exist if you want me to exist... The border is in you...

Little Clown ended his monologue with tears in his eyes. He saw the confused faces of his roommates and he told them, "*compañeros*, this *cuícatl* for the great part was recuperated from my dreams." He got a lump in his throat and started walking through the orchards without knowing exactly where to go. After six years, Little Clown finally had decided to abandon the Ranch House. The Ranch House of his *Pueblo Trabajador*.

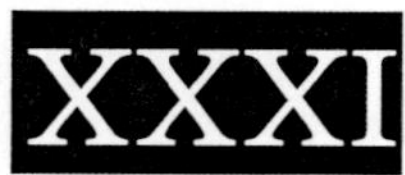

The Death of Mateo, the Atheist Monk

The afternoon that Clemente Furia Jr. assassinated Mateo, the bees were flying frantically in a swarm around the August Ladies. The day before he died, Mateo had been talking to the Prof and Engine about the situation of their country, Mexico.

The Prof and Engine were two young men who had graduated from UNAM, but they had crossed the border as wetbacks because they couldn't find a job in their own country after graduation. The Prof and Engine had been living at the Ranch House for two months, and since they got there Mateo had visited them regularly.

"We've really hit the bottom, Prof. I never imagined that after getting a civil engineering degree I'd end up as a wetback working like an ass for the gringos. Damn it to hell!"

"Yep, we've got doggone bad luck. Son of a bitch country that bore us."

"Have a little faith, guys. There's nothing wrong with working in the field. Just look at Cholver and Cuerna, how much love they put into working the land. They hug her, kiss her, caress her, talk to her, sing to her, cry to her, and confess all their drunken sins to her."

"You've got a point. But they are a couple of illiterates. They don't care if they work the fields until the day they die. As if it was the land that gave birth to them. They're a couple of failures that have lost hope of ever getting out of this fucking mess," yelled Engine.

"Son of a bitch, over here nobody has any respect for us," complained the Prof. "Even all the field hands make fun of us. Man, the way they screw with you saying 'Hurry up, Prof, you're not in the university any more. Here you're gonna get some calluses on those hands.'"

"And how about in Mexico? What do they say there?" Mateo interrupted, questioning him. "How many times did I hear, look at him, studyin' for the Church, goin' around readin' books that he says are politics, but they're probably Satan's work."

"You're right. All my neighbors started to criticize me. They would say, look at the big college graduate, now he's a taxi driver, now he's selling tacos, now he's lugging crates at the Merced, now he's selling old junk. So what did it get him to go to school all those years? What did his parents get for all the sacrifices they made to pay his tuition?"

"What a bitch! Here or there, it's the same damn thing. Fucking shitty system," responded the Prof, clearly upset.

"In our country, just like in most of them, the system is rotten through," commented Mateo. "There are millions of professionals like yourselves without a decent job because there are thousands of bastards sitting in the cushy corporate jobs who bought their degree on the black market. In our country you can do anything as long as you pay the right person. Everything is under the table. Our government is a traitor, selling our country to the highest bidders."

"The Monk is right! The government of Mexico is a traitor selling off the nation. Look how cheaply he sold us off. Our own country is selling us to the fucking gringos for twenty dollars a day," declared the Prof enthusiastically.

"It's about time that the Mexican government does something for the people. It's time that they start creating jobs and bring the value of the peso in line with the dollar," shouted Engine, as if he were at a protest.

"Sand from the scorching south, asking for white camellias," thoughtfully Mateo recited a couple lines from a poet he read frequently. "The day that the peso is in line with the dollar, I'll cut off one of my balls and half of the other one. We have more chance of being hit by lightning that of the peso being worth the same as the dollar. You might as well say that some day the continental United States is going to join up and be a part of an American Union. Impossible. I don't believe I'll live to see the day."

In the Ranch House yard, Chicho was banging hard on the side of an old bucket with a piece of metal. Chicho's intention was to make noise to draw away the cloud of bees that were buzzing around a cluster of flowers in the August Ladies orchard. Like a bat in the belfry, Chicho clanged and clanged away at the bucket. The bees, as if they were following orders from their queen, came together in a horde around the shutters (*?) at the Ranch House front door. The more Chicho banged on the bucket, the more the hive grew. In only a few minutes the entire front of the Ranch House was tapestried with bees. The hive swelled like bunch of grapes ready for harvest, and clusters of bees began to fall off, dissolving in the air before touching the ground.

Clemente Furia Jr. drove up to the Ranch House in search of Mateo. The Ranch House workers, who were contemplating the massive hive in wonder, when they saw Clemente didn't say a word, but simply pointed indoors to show him where Mateo was. Since Clemente Furia Jr. couldn't go in through the front door, he climbed in through a side window.

Hearing Clemente, Mateo immediately stood up. Clemente jumped right on him, fists and feet landing blows. As one, the two twisted around on the floor. Braided together, they beat each other like animals on the hardwood planks that creaked with each wallop. They got up and the two of them went flying outside through a window. They fell into the Ranch House yard. They kept on rolling across the ground, swinging away at each other, until they ended up close to the enormous hive.

With a powerful clout, Mateo sent his opponent to the mat. Clemente, in pain, tried to get up, but his legs trembled like cheap imitation Jello. Mateo motioned to him to get up. Clemente jumped on Mateo, who knocked him out with a punch in the face and a kick in the gut. Clemente lost consciousness for a few seconds. When he came to, he was enraged to see the mocking laughter in the faces of his workers. Clemente Furia felt humiliated. He got up and like a burst of flame launched himself at Mateo, stabbing him three times in the stomach. Nobody even had time to see when or from where Clemente Furia Jr. pulled out the knife. The field hands, faces terrified, only saw when Mateo put his hands over his belly, trying to plug with his fingertips the pools of blood where his life was leaking away.

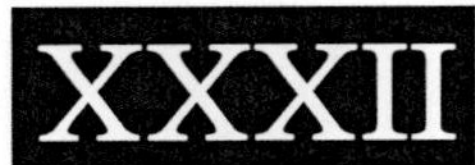

San Joaquin Packing House, Inc.

In December of 2002, Little Clown published in a Spanish-language newspaper in Los Angeles, California the following retrospective article about the impact that the 1985 amnesty program had on the San Joaquin Packing House, Inc.

The day of July 24, 1983 in the San Joaquin Valley in California saw the grand opening of the largest fruit packing factory ever constructed in the entire world, the San Joaquin Packing House, Inc. From the first day of operation, at the front entrance of the packing factory, which was an enormous glass door, a huge beehive had been forming. Mr. Glenn Jr., the owner of the factory, immediately ordered the maintenance crew to set the hive on fire. That day the wind smelled of burnt honey throughout the whole valley. That burnt honey scent would continue to appear for years, because the stubborn bees would continue to build a new hive at the factory entrance every two to three weeks, and Mr. Glenn Jr., as soon as he saw them, would become furious and immediately order to have them burned down again.

The packing house created plenty of jobs for men and women, who for the most part were Chicanos and Chicanas. The undocumented Mexicans continued to labor in the fields, and their wives would crate up fruit, but at the smaller packing houses that operated in the open air. The factory packaged fruit 24 hours a day, 365 days a year. In the factory any kind of fruit that you could imagine got packed into crates and containers. They packaged every kind of peach, plum, grape, apple, kiwi, pomegranate, persimmon, orange, lime, pear, cherry, and watermelon that there was.

Many of the undocumented women longed for the chance to one day work at the San Joaquin Packing House, Inc. It was a novelty to hear that the factory was giving away fingernail clippers to the Chicanas who worked there, as well as barrettes for keeping their hair back. They couldn't believe that the women were allowed to work in full makeup. It was a real dream for the undocumented women to be able to work some day in a clean space, with air conditioning, and the most tantalizing thing was that if they would work more than eight hours a day, they would be paid time and a half.

The working in the factory turned into a kind of lottery game for the undocumented women. Little by little they started working their way into the company, but they had to pay for their place. The Chicanas would let them take their places if they gave them money. There were women that paid up to two thousand dollars for a spot. Foremen and supervisors knew about it but turned a blind eye because they were Chicanos too.

Over time, many Chicanos and Chicanas began to relocate to the larger cities in search of a better job, so the demand for workers grew at the San Joaquin Packing House, Inc. Before long the factory found itself so in need they had to hire on undocumented workers, even minors. In barely three years of operation at the factory, ninety-nine percent of the employees were Mexican women without a green card. The men took longer to seek employment at the factory because they thought that work in the fields was man's work and packaging was women's work. A lot of the men considered that packaging work was only for men with fancy hairstyles and cologne. But bit by bit the men also started taking certain factory jobs—loaders, cleaners, cardboard cutters, and fasteners. The few Chicanos that were left were foremen or supervisors.

During the 80's the story changed for many of the undocumented farm workers. Many, paying a high price, were able to become temporary or permanent legal residents through the amnesty program signed into law by Ronald Reagan. But still many were unable to obtain documents because the ranchers, companies, foremen, and contractors did what they felt like doing with their workers.

The immigration reform through amnesty provided that any farm worker who had worked in the fields for more than 90 days would be able to correct their immigration status and work legally in the United States as a temporary worker or permanent resident.

The INS office asked that the field hands submit an application, passport-sized photographs, the results of a physical exam, and a letter from their employer that verified that the worker had been employed from such to such a date. The majority of the laborers were cheated, because they had to purchase a letter from the foreman for two to three thousand dollars. In some cases the foremen would end up with the greatest part of that money, and in other cases it was a deal made among the foreman, the labor contractor, and the employers.

Thousands of farm workers never managed to obtain their green card because they did not have enough money to pay for the letter, or even to pay for the processing of their application. The people who did arrange for legal documents had to pay for their photos, the medical exam, the application fee, and to top it off, there were many lawyers who took advantage of the fact that many didn't know how to read or didn't feel capable of filling out the application on their own. Such law offices would charge an exorbitant fee to help them complete the application, with the promise that their office would take care of submitting the application directly and that in this way the process would be much quicker.

When news of the amnesty program spread, millions of undocumented workers who never had worked in the fields came out from the cities trying to get a letter from an employer in the farm industry. The majority of the employers would send them to talk with their intermediaries, the labor contractors and the foremen. The foremen would get the order to sell letters at a certain price, but they would add their own surcharge, earning hundreds of dollars on each letter. Some letters were sold for up to five thousand dollars to workers who were known to never have worked in the fields at all. The amnesty program was like a gold mine for these con artists. The secretaries of the employers would type up a letter in less than five minutes. The employers would give a commission to the labor contractors, who would then give one to the foremen.

This immigration reform caused a huge wave of farm workers to move to the cities in search of better employment as soon as they received their work permit, which also created a greater demand for employees at the San Joaquin Packing House, Inc. as well as in all areas of agricultural labor. Many farm hands worked the fields during the day and then would take a late shift at the packing plant.

The San Joaquin Packing House, Inc. became famous for its high quality of fruit that was exported to all parts of the world, but also for its constant swarms of bees that massed in hordes around the glass entryway. Mr. Glenn Jr. had the solution, he would burn them down, leaving the wind of the San Joaquin Valley redolent with the scent of burnt honey.

Many changes came with the immigration reform of the amnesty program; the Border Patrol made its own reforms and thereby saved millions of dollars in salaries and sophisticated equipment. The INS required all employers to hire only legally documented workers. The employers had the responsibility to maintain in their files photocopies of each employee's Social Security card, ID card or Driver's License, and green cards. That way, the Border Patrol agents only had to choose employers out of the hat. They then would ask to view the files and would be able to fine employers up to $10,000 for each undocumented worker found to be working for their company or establishment. The business of the fine was in truth only a threat, because the employers had plenty of means at their disposal to fool the Border Patrol. What did happen was that for a time there were no more large roundups of illegal aliens laboring in the fields.

Be that as it may, the employers still found themselves needing to employ undocumented workers, and to cover their backs, they would accept copies of falsified documents. The illegals who had recently come over would buy green cards, ID, and Social Security cards on the black market. The workers would pay whatever they had to for the forged documents in order to be able to work. The employer knew, the Border Patrol knew, the INS knew, but everyone pretended that they didn't because that was in their best interest.

Compatriots who already had their residency would lend their documents to those who were just now immigrating so that they could find work. The national with legal papers would come to the hiring office and let them copy his documents, and then the next day the one who would show up to work was the national without papers. One Mexican always will help another when it comes to the job search in the United States.

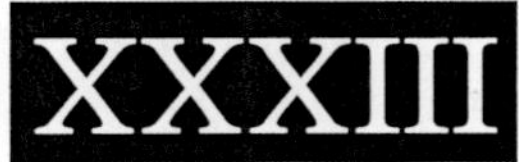

Apolonio Sánchez

Apolonio Sánchez, a 20 year-old youth, came illegally to work in the San Joaquin Packing House, Inc. A Mexican compatriot helped him to settle in. His friend paid the Coyote and found him forged documents so he could get a job at the packing house.

Apolonio started work as a feeder for the cardboard machine, but in less than two months they put him in charge of the machines that fabricated the cardboard boxes, thanks to his level of responsibility and high productivity at the job. Apolonio had graduated from high school at the Saint Nicholas Hidalgo school in Morelia, Michoacán. He was able to finish school because he had been accepted into a Student Dorm. The Morelia Student Dorms were centers that provided free room and board, paid for by the state, available only to children of farm workers.

After Apolonio finished high school, he was no longer eligible for student housing, even though he wanted to go on and enter a technical school. At the office they told him that the nest was only available for three years.

Apolonio decided to stay and live on his own in the capitol to pursue a course of study as an automobile mechanic, but to do so he would have to both work and go to school. In downtown Morelia, in front of the central cathedral, he worked mornings as a bootblack and in the afternoon he went to class. Three months later he had to give up his studies because tuition was so expensive. He continued to work shining shoes for another six months, until he decided to try his luck in the United States.

Apolonio was taught to program the cardboard box equipment, and before you could say "boo" he knew every single button and lever on the machine. In just over a year and a half Apolonio was promoted to be supervisor of the refrigeration department. He accepted the new position with pleasure. One of the Chicano workers couldn't believe that a Wetback like Apolonio was going to be a supervisor, when he didn't even speak English. The young Chicano was envious because he had wanted the job for himself. Envy rotted his heart, and one day he called the Border Patrol to turn him in. However, his accusation was not just of Apolonio, but of over ninety percent of the undocumented workers employed by the factory.

The Border Patrol agents went over the files of all the employees. They pulled out one file and set it aside. It was obvious to the agents' eyes that the files were full of falsified documents. The agents stared at Mr. Glenn Jr. The factory owner commented that these were the documents that the applicants provided when looking for a job, and that he was sorry, but he wasn't going to go and investigate as to whether the documents were forged or not. The senior agent got up from his seat with one file folder in his hand, gave Mr. Glenn Jr. a pat on the back, and told him that the situation wasn't all that bad. He half whispered that the problem was that there had been an allegation, and for that reason only they had shown up at the factory to do their duty, because otherwise they would never have bothered him. Even more softly he said that there was no reason to worry, because in his report he would state that everything was in order with the exception of one of the workers. He held out the folder with the name of Apolonio Sanchez and assured the owner that he wouldn't even have to pay a fine, because it wasn't his fault, but rather that of the worker. Mr. Glenn Jr. sighed with relief and offered to personally turn over the worker in question, but before that he invited the agents to take stroll over to the viewing platform so he could show off a little. Mr. Glenn Jr. called for his supervisors to come to the platform so he could tell them what was going on, so they in turn could inform the workers that there was no need to run from the Border Patrol agents they would see on the platform. He also ordered that Apolonio Sanchez be found and taken to his office. The supervisors went to inform the other workers, but knowing the Border Patrol as they did, knew that it must be a trap. The Border Patrol team had barely set foot on the platform when the workers took off running as if they had seen the devil himself in all his finery. Some ran through the pathways between the conveyor belts along which the fruit was rolling, and others went crazy searching for the emergency exits, running into each other in the attempt. All wound-up, Mr. Glenn Jr. begged his employees to calm down, but when he saw they were running around madly like rats in a maze, he ordered for all the exits to be locked in order to get the situation under control. The workers felt like they had been caught in a rat trap.

A pregnant woman ran to hide inside one of the refrigerated compartments. There she found Apolonio Sanchez and John Perez, one of the supervisors. The supervisor ordered Apolonio to go to Mr. Glenn Jr.'s office, but Apolonio refused to leave the refrigerated stall because he already had heard that the Border Patrol was up on the platform. John told him to turn himself in. Apolonio said no. They're looking for you. Turn yourself in. Don't be an idiot. Don't make things harder for the rest of us. Think about your fellow workers. Let the Border Patrol take you away. All of us will get together the money and send it to Tijuana so that you can pay a Coyote to cross you back into the United States, John was saying to Apolonio. Climbed up into a forklift, Apolonio shouted down to John that he was not going to turn himself in, and if what the Border Patrol wanted was him, they would have to come and get him. John stalked out angrily to tell Mr. Glenn Jr.

Apolonio saw the pregnant woman come in, and she hid herself in one of the empty fruit cartons stacked up at the entrance to the refrigerated cubicle. In order to hide her better, he used the forklift to place three fruit-filled boxes on top of the carton where the woman was. Apolonio saw a Border Patrol agent enter, and full of rage he revved up the forklift and picked up the four boxes and set them on a conveyor belt that began to take them to the exterior of the factory.

The chill of the refrigerated compartment was unbearable, and every time Apolonio or the agent would breathe they would exhale a billow of steam through their nose and mouth as if they were a couple of bulls. Five more agents entered, and between the six of them they got Apolonio to the floor and handcuffed him like a criminal. Apolonio didn't resist and let himself be led to the platform.

Apolonio saw that in one of the walled corridors lined with enormous windows they had all of his compatriots penned in. As they led Apolonio through another walkway, it occurred to him that his dream, the dream of each one of his fellow countrymen was being cut down in a mere instant by an incomprehensible twist of fate.

Apolonio didn't know that the human herd of his countrymen behind the glass was not going to be deported. They really did want only him. Thoughts flew through Apolonio's mind. He envisioned himself starving to death on the border. He thought of the dividing line of the border as a slice down one of his eyeballs. The mere thought of the border gave him chills. He felt as if the border were something like a human brain. Inside his head he saw coming slowly toward him a human shadow with a scalpel in his hand. He cried out, feeling like the two hemispheres of his brain were being sliced into. Seeing his own brain cut in two, he felt his body going limp and sideways like a puppet when its strings are dropped.

Apolonio kept on trudging down the window-framed hallway. The border would be waiting for him tomorrow, that limbo in the middle of the desert. The border was waiting for him anxiously, a bubble of dreams between the north and the south.

Apolonio couldn't accept his bad luck, or the bad luck of his fellow Mexicans. No, not he. Apolonio didn't resign himself to his fate, even though he felt humiliated at being treated like a criminal and at seeing his countrymen incarcerated like prisoners of war behind the glass.

Outside the huge picture window the bees were crashing into the glass, falling dying to the ground. Apolonio stared at the bees. His gaze stopped seeing the windowpane. Through the pane you could see a square orchard of August Lady peaches, but Apolonio saw something more. Apolonio saw swarms of bees coming and smashing against the windows of the packing plant. They were bees that had been flying since time immemorial.

Apolonio paused for a moment in the hallway, and the Border Patrol agent pulled harder on his handcuffs. Apolonio turned to see all his co-workers and then looked outside where the bees continued to commit suicide against the glass of the front factory door. Apolonio wrenched himself free from the INS agent and started running as fast as he could toward the enormous windows at the entrance. His entire self was bathed in blood as he crashed into the windowpane. You could only see a cloud of red dust, and his whole body was enveloped in shards of glass.

The alarm system went off, and all the workers without green cards shoved past the Border Control team and escaped out into the orchards. The agents didn't even bother to follow them. Rather, they went and opened all the exits so that everyone could flee.

An ambulance came to take away the body of Apolonio Sanchez. At the factory entrance, the bee hive kept growing like a bunch of grapes near bursting. The police, the Border Patrol, and Mr. Glenn Jr. came to an understanding so that everything that happened would stay their little secret.

The swelling hive kept on growing. Nobody could explain where so many bees came from. Two of the supervisors called Mr. Glenn Jr. over to take a look at the enormous hive.

"Oh my God! We've got to call the termite company right away so that they can get rid of these damned bees once and for all."

Mr. Glenn Jr. sat down for a minute to wipe his brow as he was drinking a Coca-Cola. From his seat he could see how quickly the hive was ballooning out. He got up and once more went outside to stare at the huge swarm. The limpid gaze of his blue-green eyes drew him too close to the buzzing horde. From the roof of his factory a gigantic cluster of bees detached itself from the bunch and enveloped the puffy pink flesh of his body.

Mr. Glenn Jr.'s widow, furious, ordered that all the clusters of bees hanging from the roof around the entire factory be burnt down. The breezes of the San Joaquin Valley wafted the scent of burnt honey for hundreds of miles around. The scent floated over to the schoolhouse of a small village where Little Clown was working as a bilingual education teacher with immigrants. His eyes clouded with sadness, Little Clown gazed out at the horizon through the glass panes of the window. He sighed. A strong smell of burnt honey hit him all the way down into his lungs. He stood there perplexed, going over thousands of memories from his past. He saw coming toward him a bee, flying in fits and starts as if it was injured. Before the bee could crash into the window, Little Clown grabbed off his desk a copy of the novel *Burnt Honey* and threw it as hard as he could at the window; opening forever the window of his classroom and of his heart.

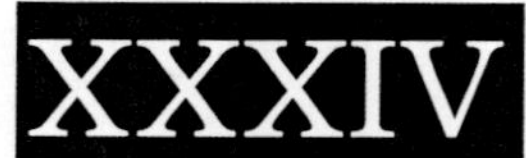

Clemente Furia Jr.

Clemente Furia Jr. was arrested by the police in a bar in Parlier, California, for the murder by stabbing of Mateo Garcia Rodriguez. Clemente had been waiting for them for weeks already, and when he saw them he held out his arms for the handcuffs. Ever since the day he had killed Mateo he had gone into hiding in the bar, where he would drink himself into a stupor. The bartender would toss him out on his ass in the wee hours of the morning, and later that day he would walk back in under his own steam. Clemente Furia Jr. never thought about the murder he had committed. No way. He didn't think about that at all. Clemente did nothing but think about his memories of Alma. Almita, Almita…

The police handcuffed Clemente Furia Jr. and then threw him to the ground and started kicking the shit out of him like he was a rabid dog. Clemente almost passed out, but he survived the beating thanks to the refuge he had created in his mind, the refuge of his Alma. Almita, Almita… From the day when Clemente Furia Sr. had taken him out of school to go pick garlic, his memories of Alma had always been his armor. One of the policemen chucked him in a cell, booting him three more times, and Clemente just curled himself into a ball with his memories.

One Mexican killed another Mexican, said a voice in a private courtroom session. It's a clear case of one Mexican killing another one. It's a case where neither one of them, neither the killed nor the killer, has a single soul who cares about them, another voice was heard to say. It's one Wetback killing another Wetback in a drunken brawl. There's nothing to prove the killer is an American citizen. He's a Wetback, yelled another voice. Clemente Furia Jr. is a Wetback who spilled the blood of another Wetback on American soil and should pay for what he has done with his life. He's a murderer. He should go to the electric chair right now, shouted another voice. Clemente Furia Jr. is neither a United States citizen nor a Mexican by birth, because he was born on the border. That being the situation, I consider this case closed. There was no murder here. The body of the victim already has been sent to his relatives in Mexico, right? Let's just forget about this case, ladies and gentlemen. Let's save our tax money. We'll save the state a few dollars. We're going to send Clemente Furia Jr. back to the border, where he was born. Let the Mexicans deal with him pronounced Judge Alma García, now Mrs. Jones.

After a long discussion the entire jury agreed to let Clemente Furia Jr. go at the border between Mexico and the United States, but with the condition that he never again set foot on United States soil for the rest of his life. Never, ever. Never again for any reason, for any motive, or under any circumstance. They warned him that if he did, they would throw him in prison for life or they would put him in the electric chair.

Judge Alma Jones refused to see the accused face to face and went to her chambers immediately with the excuse of having a terrible headache.

The next day they opened the gate of a huge barbed wire fence on the border between Mexico and the United States. Clemente Furia Jr. stepped out of a patrol car, guarded by four Border Control agents. They led him over to the door that divided the two countries, two cultures, two histories, one destiny. Perhaps the life or the death of Clemente Furia Jr.? His life was split in two. He had never lived in Mexico. They removed the handcuffs from his wrists and with a shove put him on "the other side." Clemente Furia Jr. was free, but he didn't dare take a step onto Mexican soil. Why wasn't he thrilled to be let go? Clemente's feet wouldn't come unstuck from the earth. He couldn't move. He felt as if his feet were two enormous metal bars driven down into a vat of sand.

He turned around for the last time toward the north, and his mind became clouded with the bitter and unmistakable scent of garlic. He looked toward the couth and felt imprisoned by all the freedom taken in with his gaze of stone. That rocky stare of his brown eyes was lost forever in a mirage of water in the desert that awaited him with open arms.

Glossary of terms in Spanish, Pocho and Nahuatl

Alma, Almita: The name of Clemente Furia Jr.'s childhood love, which literally means "soul," is rife with symbolic meaning.

Al rato, al ratón: Spanish or Pocho for "in a little while." The second phrase adds the word play element of "ratón", or rat, to replace "rato," or "a while."

Aztlán: The promised land of the Aztecs, the place from whence they emigrated to what is now Mexico, and to where they may return one day. The Chicano Movement recuperated the myth of Aztlán and speculated that it existed on the western coast of the United States, in what now is the state of California; thus, referring to Aztlán brings to mind the glory of a past civilization, the hope of a better tomorrow, and the 1848 Treaty with Mexico that ceded California and other territories to the United States.

Bracero(s): From the Spanish word "brazo" meaning "arm" this term refers to manual laborers. Also the term may refer to participants in the United States Bracero Program, instituted August 4, 1942, which brought experienced farm workers from Mexico on contract to work for pre-established periods of time in the United States agricultural industry. When the program ended in 1963, 12,127 guest workers had participated.

Bueno; buen trabajo: Spanish for "good"; "good work" or "good job".

Burra: A female donkey. Several popular sayings utilize the figure of the *burra* or *burro*, to work as hard as a *burro*, to be as stupid as a *burro*, or to be as docile as a *burra*.

Califas: California

Calli: Calli, also referred to as Telpuchcalli, literally meaning "house of youth," were the Aztec boys' schools.

Calmao, ese: Pocho for "calm down, dude."

Cahuitl: Nahuat term meaning time.

Chela: Pocho term for a cold beer.

Chicano: A Mexican-American who has developed an identity not tied completely to one culture or another, a hybrid U.S. ethnic identity. Many times, taking the identity of Chicano suggests an affiliation with the Chicano Movement (est. 1960s), which focuses on ethnic pride and human rights. However, often in this novel *chicano* is used to refer to the generations of Mexican youth who leave for the United States to work and change or assimilate to the extent that they are obviously different from their Mexican compatriots, in terms of dress, language use, and value system.

Chingón: A vulgar expression similar to "Badass," meaning valiant and unbeatable.

Comadre, compadre: Spanish for "co-mother" and "co-father." The relationship of *comadrazco* and *compadrazco* is similar to, yet more intense than, that of godparents in the United States.

Compañero: Literally "companion," often used to mean anything from "sir" to "buddy" to "friend," this word has strong socialist or unionist connotations. The significance is that all people are valued equally as fellow-workers and companions in a struggle.

Coyote: An individual who is wily enough to bring illegal immigrants across the border from Mexico to the United States. Although some coyotes would specialize in simple border crossings, some (like Chito in this novel) regularly contracted with U.S. employers to bring workers for a predetermined fee.

Cuícatl: Nahuat term for "poem," or as explained in the novel, "a dialogue with the heart."

Échate: Pocho for "give" or "throw out," here about equivalent to "bust out with."

El Norte: See Norte.

Ése: Spanish for "that one," in Pocho terminology this is a direct address meaning "guy" or "dude."

Gabachos: A slightly negative term for Anglo-American.

Gringo: Another term for Anglo-American, *gringo* also can carry negative connotations.

Güachar the rucas: Pocho for "watch the good-looking women."

Hijos de puta: Spanish for "sons of a bitch."

Huevonada: A severe muscle spasm, the *huevonada* is believed by Mexican immigrant workers to be a severe nerve condition that only can be relieved through a semi-spiritual ritual striking or switching with the right kind of stick.

Huizache: Bushes native to the arid climate of Michoacán, Mexico. One of the over one hundred species of acacia, this type has abundant spiny branches.

Ixpapalotl: Aztec earth mother symbol, or goddess of the butterflies, as indicated in the novel.

Jauja: A mythical place believed to be a Garden of Eden where one could live the good life, without problems or difficulties. Spanish writer Lope de Rueda immortalized the city name by recreating it as a fictional paradise in one of his plays after hearing exaggerated accounts of the natural beauty, serenity, and prosperity of the Peruvian town Jauja.

La migra: A shortened form of the word "immigration," usually signifying the Border Patrol agents who came in teams to round up illegal immigrants at their work places.

Lazarillo: The protagonist o the classic Spanish picaresque novel (anonymous) Lazarillo de Tormes, in which the central character knows no father, and perforce takes the name of the river Tormes as his progenitor.

Loco(s): Spanish for "crazy."

Mañana: Spanish for "tomorrow."

Mi Pueblo Trabajador: Literally, "my hardworking people." The word "pueblo" can signify either town or people, with the specific meaning of compatriots. "Trabajador" also conveys the connotation of working class, so does not suggest the same level of identification with the rich and aristocratic of Mexico.

Mole: Related to the Spanish verb *moler*, to grind or mash with a mortar and pestle, most commonly *mole* refers to a cooking sauce made from hot red peppers, peanuts, and chocolate.

Norte: Norte, or El Norte, literally means "North" or "The North" and usually refers to the United States.

Paisano: Literally "compatriot," here this means "fellow Mexicans."

Pa' todos los camarones: Incorporating the word play of *camarones* (shrimp) for *camaradas* (guys, buddies), this is slang Spanish meaning "for all the guys,"

Pinche: Spanish vulgar term best translated as "damned" or "fucking."

Pocho: A Mexican-American regional dialect of Spanish, this term sometimes used as an insult, meaning that the individual is not "pure" or does not speak "pure Spanish."

Purépecha: Original term for the indigenous lands and people of Michoacán, also called Tarasco by the Spanish colonizers.

Quetzacóatl: The Aztec feathered serpent god, creator of the world.

Raza: *La Raza* is a term denoting ethnic pride in the mixture of Spanish and indigenous blood that resulted in a mixed "race." The word is often used in conjunction with the struggle for equal rights.

Simón, ese: Simón is Spanish for the proper name Simon, which in Mexico is used as a word play for "yes," as it is an elongation of the Spanish "sí." The full expression is Pocho for "sure, dude."

Teaomoxtli: Ancient chronicles of Mexico, especially the Toltecs.

Telpuchcalli: See *calli.*

Tepeyac: Near contemporary Mexico City, and the ancient Aztec city of Tenochtitlán, Tepeyac originally was the site of an important shrine dedicated to Tonantzin, and today is the home of the largest cathedral honoring the Virgin of Guadalupe, the dark-skinned virgin Mary.

Tihuí: The sound of a bird song in Nahuatl, this term also can mean "let's go" in Spanish.

Tlailotlaques: An indigenous people of the time of the Aztecs.

Tlalticpac: Nahuatl term for "Earth."

Tlaloc: Tlalóc is the Aztec Rain God. Interestingly, Tlalóc is gendered male while rain is falling, and then after the rain stops, when the water standing on the ground begins to swell the seeds of the crops, to run in rivulets toward the rivers, the god is gendered female.

Tonantzin: The Aztec Goddess of motherhood, Tonantzin's pyramid existed just about where Virgin of Guadalupe was said to appear, and where now exists the famous Basilica in the Virgin's name.

UNAM: The National Autonomous University of Mexico, located in the capital, Mexico City.

Vatos: Pocho term for "dudes" or "guys."

Ya se acabó el pedo: Pocho slang expression for "and it's all taken care of."